I0004765

PUBLISHER COMMENTARY

This DoD Instruction adopts the term "cybersecurity" as it is defined in National Security Presidential Directive-54/Homeland Security Presidential Directive-23 (Reference (m)) to be used throughout DoD instead of the term "information assurance (IA)." It also establishes the positions of DoD principal authorizing official (PAO) (formerly known as principal accrediting authority) and the DoD Senior Information Security Officer (SISO) (formerly known as the Senior Information Assurance Officer) and continues the DoD Information Security Risk Management Committee (DoD ISRMC) (formerly known as the Defense Information Systems Network (DISN)/Global Information Grid (GIG) Flag Panel).

DoD's computer networks have always been targeted for cyber-attacks and now that includes the building controls systems (BCS). Defending a BCS is not as simple at protecting an IT network because most BCS consist of analog equipment that is decades old and retrofit to accept commands from modern digital controllers. Many BCS installations are a hodgepodge of technologies that should have been replaced years ago. DoD is well ahead of industry in this area because DoD recognizes it's a problem whereas most companies are blissfully unaware of their vulnerabilities.

Each of the books we publish includes a list of cybersecurity publications produced by the National Institute of Standards and Technology (NIST), Unified Facilities Criteria (UFC), Mil Handbooks and other publications that are directly applicable to the topic for consideration during the planning process. These publications cover a wide range of cybersecurity concepts that are carefully designed to work together to produce a holistic approach to cybersecurity primarily for government agencies and constitute the best practices used by industry. This holistic strategy to cybersecurity covers the gamut of security subjects from development of secure encryption standards for communication and storage of information while at rest to how best to recover from a cyber-attack.

Why buy a book you can download for free?

Some documents are only distributed in <u>electronic media</u>. Some online docs are missing some pages or the graphics are barely legible. When a new standard is released, an engineer prints it out, punches holes and puts it in a 3-ring binder. While this is not a big deal for a 5 or 10-page document, many cyber documents are over 100 pages and printing a large document is a time-consuming effort. So, an engineer that's paid $75 an hour is spending hours simply printing out the tools needed to do the job. That's time that could be better spent doing engineering. We publish these documents so engineers can focus on what they were hired to do – engineering.

A list of **Cybersecurity Standards** is attached at the end of this document.

CyberSecurity Standards Library™

Get a Complete Library of Over 300 Cybersecurity Standards on 1 Convenient DVD!

The **4th Watch CyberSecurity Standards Library** is a DVD disc that puts over 300 current and archived cybersecurity standards from NIST, DOD, DHS, CNSS and NERC at your fingertips! Many of these cybersecurity standards are hard to find and we included the current version and a previous version for many of them. The DVD includes four books written by Luis Ayala: **The Cyber Dictionary, Cybersecurity Standards, Cyber-Security Glossary of Building Hacks and Cyber-Attacks**, and **Cyber-Physical Attack Defenses: Preventing Damage to Buildings and Utilities**.

- ✓ DVD includes many Hard-to-find Cybersecurity Standards - some still in Draft.
- ✓ Docs are organized by source and listed numerically so each standard is easy to locate.
- ✓ The listing of standards on the DVD includes an abstract of the subject, and date issued.
- ✓ PDF format for use on PC, Mac, eReaders, or tablets.
- ✓ No need for WiFi / Internet.
- ✓ Save countless hours of searching and downloading.
- ✓ Carry in a briefcase - terrific for travel.

4th Watch Publishing is releasing the CyberSecurity Standards Library DVD to make it easier for you to access the tools you need to ensure the security of your computer networks and SCADA systems. We also publish many of these standards on demand so you don't need to waste valuable time searching for the latest version of a standard, printing hundreds of pages and punching holes so they can go in a three-ring binder. **Order on Amazon.com**

The DVD works on PC and Mac with the standards in PDF format. To view the CyberSecurity Standards Library on the DVD, a computer with a DVD drive is required. The most current version of your internet browser, at least 2GB of RAM, and current version of Adobe Reader is recommended. (Compatible browsers include Internet Explorer 8+, Mozilla Firefox 4+, Apple Safari 5+, Google Chrome 15+)

Department of Defense
INSTRUCTION

NUMBER 8500.01
March 14, 2014

DoD CIO

SUBJECT: Cybersecurity

References: See Enclosure 1

1. <u>PURPOSE</u>. This instruction:

a. Reissues and renames DoD Directive (DoDD) 8500.01E (Reference (a)) as a DoD Instruction (DoDI) pursuant to the authority in DoDD 5144.02 (Reference (b)) to establish a DoD cybersecurity program to protect and defend DoD information and information technology (IT).

b. Incorporates and cancels DoDI 8500.02 (Reference (c)), DoDD C-5200.19 (Reference (d)), DoDI 8552.01 (Reference (e)), Assistant Secretary of Defense for Networks and Information Integration (ASD(NII))/DoD Chief Information Officer (DoD CIO) Memorandums (References (f) through (k)), and Directive-type Memorandum (DTM) 08-060 (Reference (l)).

c. Establishes the positions of DoD principal authorizing official (PAO) (formerly known as principal accrediting authority) and the DoD Senior Information Security Officer (SISO) (formerly known as the Senior Information Assurance Officer) and continues the DoD Information Security Risk Management Committee (DoD ISRMC) (formerly known as the Defense Information Systems Network (DISN)/Global Information Grid (GIG) Flag Panel).

d. Adopts the term "cybersecurity" as it is defined in National Security Presidential Directive-54/Homeland Security Presidential Directive-23 (Reference (m)) to be used throughout DoD instead of the term "information assurance (IA)."

2. <u>APPLICABILITY</u>

a. This instruction applies to:

(1) OSD, the Military Departments, the Office of the Chairman of the Joint Chiefs of Staff (CJCS) and the Joint Staff, the Combatant Commands, the Office of the Inspector General of the DoD, the Defense Agencies, the DoD Field Activities, and all other organizational entities within the DoD (referred to collectively in this instruction as the "DoD Components").

(2) All DoD IT.

(3) All DoD information in electronic format.

(4) Special access program (SAP) information technology, other than SAP ISs handling sensitive compartmented information (SCI) material.

b. Nothing in this instruction alters or supersedes the existing authorities and policies of the Director of National Intelligence (DNI) regarding the protection of SCI as directed by Executive Order 12333 (Reference (n)) and other laws and regulations.

3. POLICY. It is DoD policy that:

a. Risk Management

(1) DoD will implement a multi-tiered cybersecurity risk management process to protect U.S. interests, DoD operational capabilities, and DoD individuals, organizations, and assets from the DoD Information Enterprise level, through the DoD Component level, down to the IS level as described in National Institute of Standards and Technology (NIST) Special Publication (SP) 800-39 (Reference (o)) and Committee on National Security Systems (CNSS) Policy (CNSSP) 22 (Reference (p)).

(2) Risks associated with vulnerabilities inherent in IT, global sourcing and distribution, and adversary threats to DoD use of cyberspace must be considered in DoD employment of capabilities to achieve objectives in military, intelligence, and business operations.

(3) All DoD IT will be assigned to, and governed by, a DoD Component cybersecurity program that manages risk commensurate with the importance of supported missions and the value of potentially affected information or assets.

(4) Risk management will be addressed as early as possible in the acquisition of IT and in an integrated manner across the IT life cycle.

(5) Documentation regarding the security posture of DoD IS and PIT systems will be made available to promote reciprocity as described in DoDI 8510.01 (Reference (q)) and to assist authorizing officials (AOs) (formerly known as designated approving or accrediting authorities) from other organizations in making credible, risk-based decisions regarding the acceptance and use of systems and the information that they process, store, or transmit.

b. Operational Resilience. DoD IT will be planned, developed, tested, implemented, evaluated, and operated to ensure that:

(1) Information and services are available to authorized users whenever and wherever required according to mission needs, priorities, and changing roles and responsibilities.

(2) Security posture, from individual device or software object to aggregated systems of systems, is sensed, correlated, and made visible to mission owners, network operators, and to the DoD Information Enterprise consistent with DoDD 8000.01 (Reference (r)).

(3) Whenever possible, technology components (e.g., hardware and software) have the ability to reconfigure, optimize, self-defend, and recover with little or no human intervention. Attempts made to reconfigure, self-defend, and recover should produce an incident audit trail.

c. Integration and Interoperability

(1) Cybersecurity must be fully integrated into system life cycles and will be a visible element of organizational, joint, and DoD Component IT portfolios.

(2) Interoperability will be achieved through adherence to DoD architecture principles, adopting a standards-based approach, and by all DoD Components sharing the level of risk necessary to achieve mission success.

(3) All interconnections of DoD IT will be managed to minimize shared risk by ensuring that the security posture of one system is not undermined by vulnerabilities of interconnected systems.

d. Cyberspace Defense. Cyberspace defense will be employed to protect, detect, characterize, counter, and mitigate unauthorized activity and vulnerabilities on DoD information networks. Cyberspace defense information will be shared with all appropriately cleared and authorized personnel in support of DoD enterprise-wide situational awareness.

e. Performance

(1) Implementation of cybersecurity will be overseen and governed through the integrated decision structures and processes described in this instruction.

(2) Performance will be measured, assessed for effectiveness, and managed relative to contributions to mission outcomes and strategic goals and objectives, in accordance with Sections 11103 and 11313 of Title 40, United States Code (U.S.C.) (Reference (s)).

(3) Data will be collected to support reporting and cybersecurity management activities across the system life cycle.

(4) Standardized IT tools, methods, and processes will be used to the greatest extent possible to eliminate duplicate costs and to focus resources on creating technologically mature and verified solutions.

f. DoD Information. All DoD information in electronic format will be given an appropriate level of confidentiality, integrity, and availability that reflects the importance of both information sharing and protection.

g. <u>Identity Assurance</u>

(1) Identity assurance must be used to ensure strong identification, authentication, and eliminate anonymity in DoD IS and PIT systems.

(2) DoD will public key-enable DoD ISs and implement a DoD-wide Public Key Infrastructure (PKI) solution that will be managed by the DoD PKI Program Management Office in accordance with DoDI 8520.02 (Reference (t)).

(3) Biometrics used in support of identity assurance will be managed in accordance with DoDD 8521.01 (Reference (u)).

h. <u>Information Technology</u>

(1) All IT that receives, processes, stores, displays, or transmits DoD information will be acquired, configured, operated, maintained, and disposed of consistent with applicable DoD cybersecurity policies, standards, and architectures.

(2) Risks associated with global sourcing and distribution, weaknesses or flaws inherent in the IT, and vulnerabilities introduced through faulty design, configuration, or use will be managed, mitigated, and monitored as appropriate.

(3) Cybersecurity requirements must be identified and included throughout the lifecycle of systems including acquisition, design, development, developmental testing, operational testing, integration, implementation, operation, upgrade, or replacement of all DoD IT supporting DoD tasks and missions.

i. <u>Cybersecurity Workforce</u>

(1) Cybersecurity workforce functions must be identified and managed, and personnel performing cybersecurity functions will be appropriately screened in accordance with this instruction and DoD 5200.2-R (Reference (v)), and qualified in accordance with DoDD 8570.01 (Reference (w)) and supporting issuances.

(2) Qualified cybersecurity personnel must be identified and integrated into all phases of the system development life cycle.

j. <u>Mission Partners</u>

(1) Capabilities built to support cybersecurity objectives that are shared with mission partners will be consistent with guidance contained in Reference (r) and governed through integrated decision structures and processes described in this instruction.

(2) DoD-originated and DoD-provided information residing on mission partner ISs must be properly and adequately safeguarded, with documented agreements indicating required levels of protection.

4. <u>RESPONSIBILITIES</u>. See Enclosure 2.

5. <u>PROCEDURES</u>. See Enclosure 3.

6. <u>INFORMATION COLLECTION REQUIREMENTS</u>. The DoD Federal Information Security Management Act (FISMA) Annual Report with Quarterly Updates, referred to in paragraphs 1v and 13q of Enclosure 2 and paragraph 12i of Enclosure 3 of this instruction, has been assigned report control symbol DD-CIO(A,Q)2296 in accordance with the procedures in DTM 12-004 (Reference (x)) and DoD 8910.1-M (Reference (y)).

7. <u>RELEASABILITY</u>. **Unlimited**. This instruction is approved for public release and is available on the Internet from the DoD Issuances Website at http://www.dtic.mil/whs/directives.

8. <u>EFFECTIVE DATE</u>. This instruction:

   a. Is effective March 14, 2014.

   b. Must be reissued, cancelled, or certified current within 5 years of its publication to be considered current in accordance with DoDI 5025.01 (Reference (z)).

   c. Will expire effective March 14, 2024 and be removed from the DoD Issuances Website if it hasn't been reissued or cancelled in accordance with Reference (z).

Teresa M. Takai
DoD Chief Information Officer

Enclosures
   1. References
   2. Responsibilities
   3. Procedures
Glossary

TABLE OF CONTENTS

ENCLOSURE 1: REFERENCES 8

ENCLOSURE 2: RESPONSIBILITIES 14

    DoD CIO 14
    DIRECTOR, DISA 16
    USD(AT&L) 17
    DEPUTY ASSISTANT SECRETARY OF DEFENSE FOR DT&E (DASD(DT&E)) 18
    DOT&E 19
    USD(P) 19
    USD(P&R) 19
    USD(I) 19
    DIRNSA/CHCSS 20
    DIRECTOR, DEFENSE SECURITY SERVICE (DSS) 21
    DIRECTOR, DIA 21
    DEPUTY CHIEF MANAGEMENT OFFICER (DCMO) 22
    OSD AND DoD COMPONENT HEADS 22
    CJCS 25
    COMMANDER, USSTRATCOM 25

ENCLOSURE 3: PROCEDURES 27

    INTRODUCTION 27
    RISK MANAGEMENT 27
    OPERATIONAL RESILIENCE 31
    INTEGRATION AND INTEROPERABILITY 32
    CYBERSPACE DEFENSE 33
    PERFORMANCE 34
    DoD INFORMATION 35
    IDENTITY ASSURANCE 36
    INFORMATION TECHNOLOGY 37
    CYBERSECURITY WORKFORCE 44
    MISSION PARTNERS 44
    DoD SISO 46
    DoD COMPONENT CIOs 47
    DoD RISK EXECUTIVE FUNCTION 48
    PAO 48
    AO 48
    ISOs OF DoD IT 49
    ISSM 49
    ISSO 50
    PRIVILEGED USERS (E.G. SYSTEM ADMINISTRATOR) 51
    AUTHORIZED USERS 51

GLOSSARY 52

    PART I. ABBREVIATIONS AND ACRONYMS 52
    PART II. DEFINITIONS...55

FIGURE

    1. Three-Tiered Approach to Risk Management 28
    2. DoD Information Technology...38

ENCLOSURE 1

REFERENCES

(a) DoD Directive 8500.01, "Information Assurance (IA)," October 4, 2002 (hereby cancelled)
(b) DoD Directive 5144.02, "DoD Chief Information Officer (DoD CIO)," April 22, 2013
(c) DoD Instruction 8500.2, "Information Assurance (IA) Implementation," February 6, 2003 (hereby cancelled)
(d) DoD Directive C-5200.19, "Control of Compromising Emanations (U)," May 16, 1995 (hereby cancelled)
(e) DoD Instruction 8552.01, "Use of Mobile Code Technologies in DoD Information Systems," October 23, 2006 (hereby cancelled)
(f) Assistant Secretary of Defense for Networks and Information Integration/DoD Chief Information Officer Memorandum, "Disposition of Unclassified DoD Computer Hard Drives," June 4, 2001 (hereby cancelled)
(g) Assistant Secretary of Defense for Networks and Information Integration/DoD Chief Information Officer Memorandum, "Certification and Accreditation Requirements for DoD-wide Managed Enterprise Services Procurements," June 22, 2006 (hereby cancelled)
(h) Assistant Secretary of Defense for Networks and Information Integration/DoD Chief Information Officer Memorandum, "Use of Peer-to-Peer (P2P) File-Sharing Applications Across DoD," November 23, 2004 (hereby cancelled)
(i) Assistant Secretary of Defense for Networks and Information Integration/DoD Chief Information Officer Memorandum, "Department of Defense (DoD) Guidance on Protecting Personally Identifiable Information (PII)," August 18, 2006 (hereby cancelled)
(j) Assistant Secretary of Defense for Networks and Information Integration/DoD Chief Information Officer Memorandum, "Encryption of Sensitive Unclassified Data At Rest on Mobile Computing Devices and Removable Storage Media," July 3, 2007 (hereby cancelled)
(k) Assistant Secretary of Defense for Networks and Information Integration/DoD Chief Information Officer Memorandum, "Protection of Sensitive Department of Defense (DoD) Data at Rest On Portable Computing Devices," April 18, 2006 (hereby cancelled)
(l) Directive-type Memorandum 08-060, "Policy on Use of Department of Defense (DoD) Information Systems — Standard Consent Banner and User Agreement," May 9, 2008, as amended (hereby cancelled)
(m) National Security Presidential Directive-54/Homeland Security Presidential Directive-23, "Cybersecurity Policy," January 8, 2008[1]
(n) Executive Order 12333, "United States Intelligence Activities," as amended
(o) National Institute of Standards and Technology Special Publication 800-39, "Managing Information Security Risk: Organization, Mission, and Information System View," current edition
(p) Committee on National Security Systems Policy 22, "Policy on Information Assurance Risk Management for National Security Systems," January 2012, as amended

---

[1] Document is classified TOP SECRET. To obtain a copy, fax a request to the Homeland Security Council Executive Secretary at 202-456-5158 and the National Security Council's Senior Director for Records and Access Management at 202-456-9200.

ENCLOSURE 1

(q) DoD Instruction 8510.01, "Risk Management Framework (RMF) for DoD Information Technology (IT)," March 12, 2014

(r) DoD Directive 8000.01, "Management of the Department of Defense Information Enterprise," February 10, 2009

(s) Title 40, United States Code

(t) DoD Instruction 8520.02, "Public Key Infrastructure (PKI) and Public Key (PK) Enabling," May 24, 2011

(u) DoD Directive 8521.01E, "Department of Defense Biometrics," February 21, 2008

(v) DoD 5200.2-R, "Personnel Security Program," January 1, 1987, as amended

(w) DoD Directive 8570.01, "Information Assurance (IA) Training, Certification, and Workforce Management," August 15, 2004

(x) Directive-type Memorandum 12-004, "DoD Internal Information Collections," April 24, 2012, as amended

(y) DoD 8910.1-M, "DoD Procedures for Management of Information Requirements," June 30, 1998

(z) DoD Instruction 5025.01, "DoD Directives Program," September 26, 2012, as amended

(aa) Title 44, United States Code

(ab) DoD Directive 5230.11, "Disclosure of Classified Military Information to Foreign Governments and International Organizations," June 16, 1992

(ac) DoD Directive 8115.01, "Information Technology Portfolio Management," October 10, 2005

(ad) DoD Instruction 5205.13, "Defense Industrial Base (DIB) Cyber Security/Information Assurance (CS/IA) Activities," January 29, 2010

(ae) DoD Directive 3020.40, "DoD Policy and Responsibilities for Critical Infrastructure," January 14, 2010, as amended

(af) Deputy Secretary of Defense Memorandum, "Delegation of Authority to Negotiate and Conclude International Agreements on Cooperation in Information Assurance and Computer Network Defense," March 5, 2002[2]

(ag) DoD Directive 5530.3, "International Agreements," June 11, 1987, as amended

(ah) Joint DoD/Intelligence Community memorandum, "Establishment of a Department of Defense (DoD)/Intelligence Community (IC) Unified Cross Domain Management Office (UCDMO)," July 15, 2006

(ai) Unified Cross Domain Management Office Charter, March 21, 2007

(aj) Assistant Secretary of Defense for Networks and Information Integration/DoD Chief Information Officer Memorandum/Commander, U.S. Strategic Command Memorandum, "Establishment of the Department of Defense Enterprise-wide Information Assurance and Computer Network Defense Solutions Steering Group," September 11, 2003

(ak) National Security Directive 42, "National Policy for the Security of National Security Telecommunications and Information Systems," July 5, 1990

(al) Office of Management and Budget Circular A-130, "Management of Federal Information Resources," as amended

(am) Chairman of the Joint Chiefs of Staff Instruction 6211.02, "Defense Information System Network (DISN) Responsibilities," current edition

(an) DoD Instruction 8551.1, "Ports, Protocols, and Services Management (PPSM)," August 13, 2004

---

[2] Requests for copies can be forwarded to the DoD CIO.

ENCLOSURE 1

(ao) DoD Instruction 8100.04, "DoD Unified Capabilities (UC)," December 9, 2010

(ap) Charter Defense Information Systems Network Security Accreditation Working Group, March 26, 2004[2]

(aq) Defense Information System Network Global Information Grid Flag Panel Charter, April 2012, as amended[2]

(ar) DoD Directive 5134.01, "Under Secretary of Defense for Acquisition, Technology, and Logistics (USD(AT&L))," December 9, 2005, as amended

(as) DoD Instruction 3200.12, "DoD Scientific and Technical Information Program (STIP)," August 22, 2013

(at) DoD Instruction 8580.1, "Information Assurance (IA) in the Defense Acquisition System," July 9, 2004

(au) DoD Directive 5000.01, "The Defense Acquisition System," May 12, 2003

(av) Interim DoD Instruction 5000.02, "Operation of the Defense Acquisition System," November 25, 2013

(aw) DoD Instruction 4630.8, "Procedures for Interoperability and Supportability of Information Technology (IT) and National Security Systems (NSS)," June 30, 2004

(ax) Section 1043 of Public Law 106-65, "Information Assurance Initiative," October 5, 1999

(ay) DoD Instruction 5200.39, "Critical Program Information (CPI) Protection within the Department of Defense," July 16, 2008, as amended

(az) DoD Instruction 5134.16, "Deputy Assistant Secretary of Defense for Systems Engineering (DASD(SE))," August 19, 2011

(ba) DoD 8570.01-M, "Information Assurance Workforce Improvement Program," December 19, 2005, as amended

(bb) DoD Instruction 5134.17, "Deputy Assistant Secretary of Defense for Developmental Test and Evaluation (DASD(DT&E))," October 25, 2011

(bc) Director, Operational Test and Evaluation Memorandum, "Procedures for Operational Test and Evaluation of Information Assurance in Acquisition Programs," January 21, 2009[3]

(bd) Director, Operational Test and Evaluation Memorandum, "Clarification of Procedures for Operational Test and Evaluation of Information Assurance in Acquisition Programs," November 4, 2010[4]

(be) Director, Operational Test and Evaluation Memorandum, "Test and Evaluation of Information Assurance in Acquisition Programs," February 1, 2013

(bf) DoD Directive 5100.20, "National Security Agency/Central Security Service (NSA/CSS)," January 26, 2010

(bg) Committee on National Security Systems Policy 11, "National Policy Governing the Acquisition of Information Assurance (IA) and IA-Enabled Information Technology Products," June 2013, as amended

(bh) Title 10, United States Code

(bi) Committee on National Security Systems Policy 15, "National Information Assurance Policy on the Use of Public Standards for the Secure Sharing of Information Among National Security Systems," October 1, 2012

(bj) DoD 5220.22-M, "National Industrial Security Program Operating Manual," February 28, 2006, as amended

---

[3] Available at http://www.dote.osd.mil/pub/policies/2009/20090121Procedure_forOTEofIAinAcqPrograms.pdf.
[4] Avalable at http://www.dote.osd.mil/pub/policies/2010/20101104Clarification_ofProcedures_forOTE_ofIA_inAcq Progs.pdf.

(bk) DoD Directive O-8530.1, "Computer Network Defense (CND)," January 8, 2001

(bl) DoD Instruction O-8530.2, "Support to Computer Network Defense (CND)," March 9, 2001

(bm) DoD Instruction 5200.44, "Protection of Mission Critical Functions to Achieve Trusted Systems and Networks (TSN)," November 5, 2012

(bn) DoD Instruction 8560.01, "Communications Security (COMSEC) Monitoring and Information Assurance (IA) Readiness Testing," October 9, 2007

(bo) DoD Manual 5200.01, Volume 3, "DoD Information Security Program: Protection of Classified Information," February 24, 2012, as amended

(bp) DoD Manual 5200.01, Volume 4, "DoD Information Security Program: Controlled Unclassified Information (CUI)," February 24, 2012

(bq) DoD 5400.11-R, "Department of Defense Privacy Program," May 14, 2007

(br) Committee on National Security Systems Instruction 1010, "24 x 7 Computer Incident Response Capability (CIRC) on National Security Systems," October 3, 2012

(bs) DoD Manual 5200.01, Volume 1, "DoD Information Security Program: Overview, Classification, and Declassification," February 24, 2012

(bt) DoD Instruction 1400.25, Volume 731, "DoD Civilian Personnel Management System: Suitability and Fitness Adjudication For Civilian Employees," August 24, 2012

(bu) Title 29, United States Code

(bv) National Institute of Standards and Technology Special Publication 800-34, Revision 1, "Contingency Planning Guide for Federal Information Systems," current edition

(bw) DoD 5200.08-R, "Physical Security Program," April 9, 2007, as amended

(bx) DoD Chief Information Officer Memorandum, "Cross Domain Support Element (CDSE) Responsibilities," October 11, 2011

(by) DoD Manual 5200.01, Volume 2, "DoD Information Security Program: Marking of Classified Information," February 24, 2012, as amended

(bz) DoD 5220.22-R, "Industrial Security Regulation," April 12, 1985

(ca) Committee on National Security Systems Policy 300, "National Policy on Control of Compromising Emanations," April 2004, as amended

(cb) Committee on National Security Systems Instruction 7000, "TEMPEST Countermeasures for Facilities," May 2004, as amended

(cc) DoD Directive 5015.2, "DoD Records Management Program," March 6, 2000

(cd) Unified Command Plan, current edition

(ce) Chairman of the Joint Chiefs of Staff Instruction 6510.01, "Information Assurance (IA) and Support to Computer Network Defense (CND)," February 9, 2011, as amended

(cf) National Institute of Standards and Technology Special Publication 800-30, "Guide for Conducting Risk Assessments," current edition

(cg) DoD Directive 5105.53, "Director of Administration and Management (DA&M)," February 26, 2008

(ch) National Institute of Standards and Technology Special Publication 800-37, "Guide for Applying the Risk Management Framework to Federal Information Systems," current edition

(ci) Committee on National Security Systems Instruction 1253, "Security Categorization and Control Selection for National Security Systems," March 15, 2012, as amended (cj) National Institute of Standards and Technology Special Publication 800-53, "Recommended Security Controls for Federal Information Systems and Organizations," current edition

(ck) National Institute of Standards and Technology Special Publication 800-53A, "Guide for Assessing the Security Controls in Federal Information Systems," current edition

(cl) Section 806 of the Ike Skelton National Defense Authorization Act for Fiscal Year 2011, January 7, 2011

(cm) DoD Directive 3020.26, "Department of Defense Continuity Programs," January 9, 2009

(cn) Secretary of Defense Memorandum, "Maintaining Readiness to Operate in Cyberspace Domain," December 7, 2012

(co) DoD Instruction 8523.01, "Communications Security (COMSEC)," April 22, 2008

(cp) National Institute of Standards and Technology Special Publication 800-126, "The Technical Specification for Security Content Automation Protocol (SCAP): SCAP Version 1.0," current edition

(cq) DoD O-8530.01-M, "Department of Defense Computer Network Defense (CND) Service Provider Certification and Accreditation Program," December 17, 2003

(cr) DoD Instruction 8410.02, "NetOps for the Global Information Grid (GIG)," December 19, 2008

(cs) National Institute of Standards and Technology Special Publication 800-137, "Information Security Continuous Monitoring," current edition

(ct) DoD Instruction 8520.03, "Identity Authentication for Information Systems," May 13, 2011

(cu) DoD Directive 5505.13E, "DoD Executive Agent (EA) for the DoD Cyber Crime Center (DC3)," March 1, 2010

(cv) DoD Instruction 5240.26, "Countering Espionage, International Terrorism, and the Counterintelligence (CI) Insider Threat," May 4, 2012, as amended

(cw) Chairman of the Joint Chiefs of Staff Instruction 3170.01, "Joint Capabilities Integration and Development System," January 10, 2012

(cx) DoD Directive 7045.14, "The Planning, Programming, Budgeting, and Execution (PPBE) Process," January 25, 2013

(cy) DoD Chief Information Officer Memorandum, "Department of Defense Chief Information Officer Executive Board Charter," July 7, 2005

(cz) DoD Instruction 5200.01, "DoD Information Security Program and Protection of Sensitive Compartmented Information," October 9, 2008, as amended

(da) DoD Instruction 8320.02, "Sharing Data Information, and Technology (IT) Services in the Department of Defense," August 5, 2013

(db) DoD 8320.02-G, "Guidance for Implementing Net-Centric Data Sharing," April 12, 2006

(dc) DoD Directive 5230.09, "Clearance of DoD Information for Public Release," August 22, 2008

(dd) DoD Instruction 8582.01, "Security of Unclassified DoD Information on Non-DoD Information Systems," June 6, 2012

(de) DoD Instruction 5400.16, "DoD Privacy Impact Assessment (PIA) Guidance," February 12, 2009

(df) DoD 8580.02-R, "DoD Health Information Security Regulation," July 12, 2007

(dg) DoD Manual 5205.02, "DoD Operations Security (OPSEC) Program Manual," November 3, 2008

ENCLOSURE 1

(dh) DoD Instruction 8550.01, "DoD Internet Services and Internet-Based Capabilities," September 11, 2012

(di) Under Secretary of Defense for Acquisition, Technology, and Logistics Memorandum, "Document Streamlining Program Protection Plan," July 18, 2011

(dj) Section 811 of Public Law 106-398, "National Defense Authorization Fiscal Year 2001," October 30, 2000

(dk) DoD Instruction 8581.01, "Information Assurance (IA) Policy for Space Systems Used by the Department of Defense," June 8, 2010

(dl) Committee on National Security Systems Instruction 4004.1, "Destruction and Emergency Protection Procedures for COMSEC and Classified Material," August 2006, as amended

(dm) National Institute of Standards and Technology Special Publication 800-88, "Guidelines for Media Sanitization," current edition

(dn) DoD Architecture Framework Version 2.02, August 2010[5]

(do) DoD Instruction 5000.64, "Accountability and Management of DoD Equipment and Other Accountable Property," May 19, 2011

(dp) DoD Instruction 2030.08, "Implementation of Trade Security Controls (TSC) for Transfers of DoD U.S. Munitions List (USML) and Commerce Control List (CCL) Personal Property to Parties Outside DoD Control," May 23, 2006

(dq) DoD Instruction 1035.01, "Telework Policy," April 4, 2012

(dr) National Institute of Standards and Technology Special Publication 800-114, "Users Guide to Securing External Devices for Telework and Remote Access," current edition

(ds) National Institute of Standards and Technology Special Publication 800-147, "Basic Input/Output System (BIOS) Protection Guidelines," current edition

(dt) Assistant Secretary of Defense for Networks and Information Integration/DoD Chief Information Officer, "Coalition Public Key Infrastructure, X.509 Certificate Policy," current edition

(du) DoD Directive 5230.20, "Visits and Assignments of Foreign Nationals," June 22, 2005

(dv) DoD Instruction 5230.27, "Presentation of DoD-Related Scientific and Technical Papers at Meetings," October 6, 1987

(dw) DoD Instruction 2040.02, "International Transfers of Technology, Articles, and Services," July 10, 2008

(dx) DoD Instruction 1100.22, "Policy and Procedures for Determining Workforce Mix," April 12, 2010

(dy) DoD Directive 5205.02E, "DoD Operations Security (OPSEC) Program," June 20, 2012

(dz) Committee on National Security Systems Instruction Number 4009, "National Information Assurance (IA) Glossary," April 26, 2010, as amended

(ea) Joint Publication 1-02, "DoD Dictionary of Military and Associated Terms," current edition

(eb) National Institute of Standards and Technology Special Publication 800-63, "Electronic Authentication Guideline," current edition

---

[5] Available at http://dodcio.defense.gov/dodaf20.aspx.

ENCLOSURE 2

RESPONSIBILITIES

1. <u>DoD CIO</u>. The DoD CIO:

   a. Monitors, evaluates, and provides advice to the Secretary of Defense regarding all DoD cybersecurity activities and oversees implementation of this instruction.

   b. Develops and establishes DoD cybersecurity policy and guidance consistent with this instruction and in accordance with applicable federal law and regulations.

   c. Appoints a DoD SISO in accordance with section 3541 of Title 44, U.S.C. (Reference (aa)).

   d. Coordinates with the Under Secretary of Defense for Policy (USD(P)) to ensure that cybersecurity strategies and policies are aligned with overarching DoD cyberspace policy and, in accordance with DoDD 5230.11 (Reference (ab)), support policies relating to the disclosure of classified military information to foreign governments and international organizations.

   e. Coordinates with the Under Secretary of Defense for Personnel and Readiness (USD(P&R)) to:

      (1) Ensure personnel identity policies and cybersecurity policies and capabilities are aligned and mutually supportive.

      (2) Develop cybersecurity workforce management policies and capabilities to support identification and qualifications for a professional cybersecurity workforce.

   f. Coordinates with the Under Secretary of Defense for Intelligence (USD(I)) to ensure that cybersecurity policies and capabilities are aligned with and mutually supportive of personnel, physical, industrial, information, and operations security policies and capabilities.

   g. Coordinates with NIST in development of cybersecurity-related standards and guidelines.

   h. Maintains a formal coordination process with the Intelligence Community (IC) Chief Information Officer (CIO) to ensure proper protection of IC information within DoD, reciprocity of IS authorization and cybersecurity risk management processes, and alignment of cybersecurity.

   i. Coordinates with the Under Secretary of Defense for Acquisition, Technology, and Logistics (USD(AT&L)) to ensure that cybersecurity responsibilities are integrated into processes for DoD acquisition programs, including research and development.

j. Coordinates with the Director, Operational Test and Evaluation (DOT&E) to ensure that cybersecurity responsibilities are integrated into the operational testing and evaluation for DoD acquisition programs.

k. Coordinates and advocates resources for DoD-wide cybersecurity solutions, including overseeing appropriations allocated to the DoD cybersecurity program.

l. Appoints a PAO for DoD ISs and PIT systems governed by the Enterprise Information Environment Mission Area (MA) (EIEMA) as described in DoDD 8115.01 (Reference (ac)).

m. Coordinates with the DoD MA owners to ensure that cybersecurity responsibilities are addressed for all DoD IT.

n. Coordinates with the USD(P) and USD(I) on integrating Defense Industrial Base (DIB) cybersecurity threat information-sharing activities and enhancing DoD and DIB cyber situational awareness in accordance with DoDI 5205.13 (Reference (ad)) and in support of DoDD 3020.40 (Reference (ae)).

o. Develops policy for negotiating, performing, and concluding agreements with international partners to engage in cooperative international cybersecurity activities, in coordination with the USD(P), USD(I), and the Director, National Security Agency (NSA)/Chief, Central Security Service (DIRNSA/CHCSS).

p. Negotiates and concludes agreements with international partners to engage in cooperative international cybersecurity and cyberspace defense activities, according to authority described in Deputy Secretary of Defense Memorandum (Reference (af)) and subject to the provisions of DoDD 5530.3 (Reference (ag)), in coordination with the:

(1) USD(P).

(2) General Counsel of the Department of Defense.

(3) Under Secretary of Defense (Comptroller)/Chief Financial Officer, Department of Defense.

(4) USD(I), when such agreements materially affect cleared industry.

(5) CJCS.

q. Establishes policy for the life cycle management of cross-domain (CD) solutions (CDSs). This policy will address shared risk, in coordination with the IC CIO and with the direct support from the DoD/IC Unified Cross Domain Management Office (UCDMO) in accordance with Joint DoD/IC Memorandum (Reference (ah)) and the UCDMO Charter (Reference (ai)).

r. Develops and implements policy regarding continuous monitoring of DoD IT with direct support from NSA/CSS and Defense Information Systems Agency (DISA), and input from the other DoD Components.

s. Appoints a military officer in the grade of O-6 or an equivalent civilian employee as the Defense IA Security Accreditation Working Group (DSAWG) Chair.

t. Develops and implements policy for cybersecurity workforce awareness, education, training, and qualification in coordination with the USD(P&R).

u. Maintains a Defense-wide view of cybersecurity resources that supports national, organizational, joint, and DoD Component cybersecurity program planning.

v. Conducts an annual assessment of DoD Component cybersecurity programs as required by section 3545 of Reference (aa).

w. Co-chairs the Enterprise-wide IA and Computer Network Defense Solutions Steering Group (ESSG) in accordance with the ASD(NII)/DoD CIO/Commander, U.S. Strategic Command Memorandum (Reference (aj)).

x. Ensures that compromising emanations (i.e., TEMPEST) countermeasures implemented within DoD comply with current national policies.

y. Ensures compliance with the requirements of National Security Directive 42 (Reference (ak)) and collaborate with the DIRNSA/CHCSS on the performance of DIRNSA/CHCSS duties, pursuant to Reference (ak), as the National Manager for National Security Telecommunications and Information Systems Security.

2. DIRECTOR, DISA. Under the authority, direction, and control of the DoD CIO and in addition to the responsibilities in section 13 of this enclosure, the Director, DISA:

a. Develops, implements, and, in coordination with Commander, U.S. Strategic Command (USSTRATCOM), manages cybersecurity for the DISN, consistent with this instruction and its supporting guidance.

b. Develops and maintains control correlation identifiers (CCIs), security requirements guides (SRGs), security technical implementation guides (STIGs), and mobile code risk categories and usage guides that implement and are consistent with DoD cybersecurity policies, standards, architectures, security controls, and validation procedures, with the support of the NSA/CSS, using input from stakeholders, and using automation whenever possible.

c. Develops or acquires solutions that support cybersecurity objectives for use throughout DoD via the ESSG process in accordance with Reference (aj).

d. Establishes and maintains the IA Support Environment (IASE) in accordance with

Office of Management and Budget Circular A-130 (Reference (al)) as the DoD knowledge repository for cybersecurity related policy, guidance, and information.

e. Oversees and maintains the connection approval process in accordance with CJCS Instruction (CJCSI) 6211.02 (Reference (am)), CD connection policy as issued by DoD CIO, DoDI 8551.01 (Reference (an)), and DoDI 8100.04 (Reference (ao)) for the DISN (e.g., the Secret Internet Protocol Router Network (SIPRNet) and the Non-Classified Internet Protocol Router Network (NIPRNet)) in coordination with the DSAWG (Reference (ap)) and DoD ISRMC (Reference (aq)), when appropriate.

f. Facilitates multinational information sharing efforts, as well as information sharing between the DoD Components and eligible foreign nations in support of approved international cybersecurity and cyberspace defense agreements.

g. Supports training, exercises, workforce development, network evaluation, and other efforts to build international partner cybersecurity and cyberspace defense capacity.

h. Provides enterprise CD services compliant with the UCDMO-managed CDS Baseline List of validated solutions posted on the SIPRNet and the Joint Worldwide Intelligence Communications System (JWICS) UCDMO Intelink sites. Working with UCDMO, integrates new CD requirements into DoD Enterprise CD services.

i. Ensures the continued development and maintenance of guidance and standards procedures to catalog, regulate, and control the use and management of Internet protocols, data services, and associated ports on DoD networks, in accordance with Reference (an).

j. Develops and provides cybersecurity training and awareness products and a distributive training capability to support the DoD Components in accordance with Reference (w) and post the training materials on the IASE Website (http://iase.disa.mil/).

k. Conducts command cyber readiness inspections and operational risk assessments in support of USSTRATCOM.

l. Coordinates with the USD(I) to ensure command cyber readiness inspection guidance and metrics provide a unity of effort among the security disciplines (i.e., personnel, physical, industrial, information, operations, and cybersecurity).

3. USD(AT&L). The USD(AT&L):

a. Integrates policies established in this instruction and its supporting guidance into acquisition policy, regulations, and guidance consistent with DoDD 5134.01 (Reference (ar)).

b. Through the Assistant Secretary of Defense for Research and Engineering, monitors and oversees all DoD cybersecurity research and engineering investments, including research at the NSA.

c. Integrates cybersecurity assessments into developmental testing and evaluation.

d. Establishes and maintains the Cybersecurity and Information Assurance Center (formerly IA Technology Analysis Center) in accordance with DoDI 3200.12 (Reference (as)).

e. Ensures that the DoD acquisition process incorporates cybersecurity planning, implementation, testing, and evaluation consistent with Reference (q), DoDI 8580.01 (Reference (at)), DoDD 5000.01 (Reference (au)), DoDI 5000.02 (Reference (av)), DoDI 4630.8 (Reference (aw)), section 1043 of Public Law 106-65 (Reference (ax)), and this instruction, in coordination with the DoD CIO.

f. Assists with acquisition-related (e.g., research, development, test and evaluation (T&E)) agreements, and international cybersecurity and cyberspace defense negotiations and agreements, in accordance with Reference (ag), as needed.

g. Ensures that PIT systems included in acquisition programs are designated, categorized, and have their authorization boundaries defined according to the guidelines provided in Reference (q).

h. Ensures that policy and procedures for developing program protection plans (PPPs) required by DoDI 5200.39 (Reference (ay)) address cybersecurity in accordance with this instruction.

i. Defines, develops, and integrates systems security engineering (SSE) into the systems engineering workforce and curriculum in accordance with DoDI 5134.16 (Reference (az)).

j. Ensures that acquisition community personnel with IT development responsibilities are qualified in accordance with Reference (w) and DoD 8570.01-M (Reference (ba)).

k. Coordinates with the DoD Test Resource Management Center (TRMC) for establishment of developmental T&E (DT&E) specific cybersecurity architectures and requirements.

4. <u>DEPUTY ASSISTANT SECRETARY OF DEFENSE FOR DT&E (DASD(DT&E))</u>. Under the authority, direction, and control of the USD(AT&L), the DASD(DT&E):

a. Exercises oversight responsibility for developmental test planning in support of interoperability and cybersecurity for programs acquiring DoD IS and PIT systems in accordance with DoDI 5134.17 (Reference (bb)).

b. Establishes procedures to ensure that cognizant DT&E authorities for acquisition programs verify that adequate DT&E to support cybersecurity is planned, resourced, documented, and can be executed in a timely manner prior to approval of program documents.

5. <u>DOT&E</u>. The DOT&E:

a. Develops and provides policy for cybersecurity testing and evaluation during operational evaluations within DoD, including, but not limited to the DOT&E Memorandum (Reference (bc)) describing the cybersecurity testing process, clarified by updates in the DOT&E Memorandums (References (bd) and (be)).

b. Conducts independent cybersecurity assessments during operational test and evaluation (OT&E) for systems under acquisition and reports the findings as part of the acquisition process.

c. Oversees cybersecurity assessments by test agencies during both acquisition and exercise events as mandated by relevant statutory requirements.

d. Reviews and approves cybersecurity OT&E documentation for all IT, IS, PIT, and special interest programs as required.

6. <u>USD(P)</u>. The USD(P):

a. Coordinates with the DoD CIO to ensure that cybersecurity strategies, policies, and capabilities are aligned with overarching DoD cyberspace policy, and are supportive of policies and capabilities relating to the disclosure of classified military information to foreign governments and international organizations in accordance with Reference (ab).

b. Coordinates with the DoD CIO on international cybersecurity and cyberspace defense strategies and policies, as well as the negotiating, performing, and concluding agreements with international partners to engage in cooperative, international cybersecurity and cyberspace defense activities in accordance with Reference (af).

c. Coordinates with the DoD CIO on enhancing DoD and DIB cyber situational awareness in accordance with Reference (ad) and in support of Reference (ae).

7. <u>USD(P&R)</u>. The USD(P&R) supports implementation of cybersecurity requirements for effective manning, management, and readiness assessment of the cybersecurity workforce in accordance with References (w) and (ba).

8. <u>USD(I)</u>. The USD(I):

a. Coordinates with the DoD CIO on development and implementation of cybersecurity policy, guidance, procedures, and controls related to personnel, physical, industrial, information and operations security.

b. Coordinates with the DoD CIO and the USD(P) on intelligence-related international cybersecurity and cyberspace defense strategies, policies, and agreements with international partners.

c. Appoints the PAO for DoD ISs and PIT systems governed by the DoD portion of the Intelligence Mission Area (DIMA) as described in Reference (ac).

9. <u>DIRNSA/CHCSS</u>. Under the authority, direction, and control of the USD(I), and in addition to the cybersecurity-related responsibilities in DoDD 5100.20 (Reference (bf)) and the responsibilities in section 13 of this enclosure, the DIRNSA/CHCSS:

a. Supports the DoD CIO by providing cybersecurity architecture and mechanisms to support Defense military, intelligence, and business functions, including but not limited to cryptography, PKI, and IS security engineering services.

b. Evaluates or validates security implementation specifications described in this instruction.

c. Provides cybersecurity support to the DoD Components in order to assess threats to, and vulnerabilities of, information technologies.

d. Engages the cybersecurity industry and DoD user community to foster development, evaluation, and deployment of cybersecurity solutions that satisfy the guidance in this instruction.

e. Provides SSE services to the DoD Components, including describing information protection needs, properly selecting and implementing appropriate security controls, and assessing the effectiveness of system security.

f. Supports the development of NIST publications and provides engineering support and other technical assistance for their implementation within DoD.

g. Develops SSE training and qualification programs and oversees continuing education requirements for all trained IS security engineers and cybersecurity architects throughout DoD in accordance with Reference (ba).

h. Serves as the DoD focal point for the National IA Partnership and establishes criteria and processes for evaluating and validating all IA and IA-enabled products in accordance with CNSSP 11 (Reference (bg)).

i. Develops and issues security implementation specifications for the configuration of IA- and IA-enabled products (e.g., security configuration guides) and supports DISA in the development of SRGs and STIGs.

j. Serves as the DoD focal point for cybersecurity cryptographic research and development in accordance with Assistant Secretary of Defense for Research and Engineering direction and in coordination with the Director, Defense Advanced Research Projects Agency.

k. Manages the DoD IA Scholarship Program in accordance with sections 2200-2200f of Title 10, U.S.C. (Reference (bh)).

l. Plans, designs, manages, and executes the development and implementation of the key management infrastructure within DoD in coordination with DoD CIO.

m. Plans, designs, and manages the development and implementation of PKI within DoD, in coordination with DoD CIO and DISA.

n. Approves all applications of cryptographic algorithms for the protection of classified information.

o. Approves all cryptography used to protect classified information in accordance with CNSSP 15 (Reference (bi)).

p. Develops, implements, and manages a cybersecurity program for layered protection of DoD cryptographic SCI systems and a cybersecurity education, training, and awareness program for users and administrators of DoD cryptographic SCI systems in accordance with applicable DoD and DNI policies and guidance.

q. Conducts risk assessments of mobile code technologies, recommends the assignment of mobile code technologies to specific risk categories, and provides technical advice and assistance in the development of countermeasures to identified risks associated with specific mobile code technology implementations.

10. <u>DIRECTOR, DEFENSE SECURITY SERVICE (DSS)</u>. Under the authority, direction, and control of the USD(I) and in addition to the responsibilities in section 13 of this enclosure, the Director, DSS, monitors and oversees IS security practices of DoD contractors and vendors processing classified DoD information in accordance with DoD 5220.22M (Reference (bj)), and DoDD O-8530.1 (Reference (bk)), and DoDI O-8530.2 (Reference (bl)).

11. <u>DIRECTOR, DEFENSE INTELLIGENCE AGENCY (DIA)</u>. Under the authority, direction, and control of the USD(I) and in addition to the responsibilities in section 13 of this enclosure, the Director, DIA:

a. Provides finished intelligence, including threat assessments, in support of cybersecurity activities.

b. Develops, implements, and manages a cybersecurity program for DoD non-cryptographic SCI systems, including the DoD Intelligence IS (DoDIIS) and JWICS.

12. <u>DEPUTY CHIEF MANAGEMENT OFFICER (DCMO)</u>. The DCMO appoints the PAO for DoD ISs and PIT systems governed by the Business Mission Area (BMA), as described in Section 2222 of Reference (aa).

13. <u>DoD COMPONENT HEADS</u>. The DoD Component heads:

    a. Ensure that IT under their purview complies with this instruction.

    b. Ensure that cybersecurity requirements are addressed and visible in all capability portfolios, IT life-cycle management processes, and investment programs incorporating IT.

    c. Appoint an AO for all DoD IS and PIT systems under their purview and ensure all DoD ISs and PIT systems are authorized in accordance with Reference (q).

    d. Ensure that PIT systems are identified, designated as such, and centrally registered at the DoD Component level.

    e. Ensure that SSE and trusted systems and networks (TSN) processes, tools, and techniques described in DoDI 5200.44 (Reference (bm)) are used in the acquisition of all applicable IT under their purview.

    f. Ensure that organizational solutions that support cybersecurity objectives acquired and developed via the ESSG process in accordance with Reference (aj) are implemented when possible, and participate in the ESSG process to ensure capabilities acquired or developed meet organizational requirements.

    g. Provide for a cybersecurity monitoring and testing capability in accordance with DoDI 8560.01 (Reference (bn)) and other applicable laws and regulations.

    h. Provide for vulnerability mitigation and incident response and reporting capabilities in order to:

        (1) Comply with mitigations as directed by Commander, USSTRATCOM orders, or other directives such as alerts and bulletins and provide support to cyberspace defense, in accordance with Reference (bl).

        (2) Limit damage and restore effective service following an incident.

        (3) Collect and keep audit data to support technical analysis relating to misuse, penetration, or other incidents involving IT under their purview, and provide this data to appropriate law enforcement (LE) or other investigating agencies.

        (4) Establish procedures to ensure prompt management action and reporting in accordance with:

(a) DoD Manual (DoDM) 5200.01, Volume 3 (Reference (bo)) for an actual or potential compromise of classified information.

(b) DoDM 5200.01, Volume 4 (Reference (bp)) for an actual or potential unauthorized disclosure of controlled unclassified information (CUI) (e.g., proprietary information, LE information).

(c) Reference (bj) when such losses occur on cleared contractor systems.

(d) DoD 5400.11-R (Reference (bq)) for a loss or unauthorized disclosure of personally identifiable information (PII) or other Privacy Act information.

(5) Comply with CNSS Instruction (CNSSI) 1010 (Reference (br)).

i. Ensure that contracts and other agreements include specific requirements to provide cybersecurity for DoD information and the IT used to process that information in accordance with this instruction.

j. Ensure that all personnel with access to DoD IT are appropriately cleared and qualified under the provisions of Reference (v) and that access to all DoD IT processing specified types of information (e.g., collateral, SCI, CUI) under their purview is authorized in accordance with the provisions of Reference (bo) and DoDM 5200.01, Volume 1 (Reference (bs)) or Reference (bp).

k. Ensure that personnel occupying cybersecurity positions are:

(1) Assigned in writing.

(2) Trained and qualified in accordance with References (w) and (ba).

(3) Assigned a position designation using the criteria found in Reference (v) and DoDI 1400.25 Vol. 731 (Reference (bt)). The position designation will be documented in the Defense Civilian Personnel Data System (DCPDS).

(4) Meet the associated suitability and fitness requirements.

l. Cybersecurity training and awareness products developed by DISA will be used to meet the baseline user awareness training required by Reference (w). DoD Components will provide additional cybersecurity orientation, training, and awareness programs to reinforce the objectives of the DoD Enterprise cybersecurity awareness programs to authorized users of ISs. This includes conducting additional in-depth training on DoD Component-specific topics.

m. Ensure that appropriate notice of privacy rights and monitoring policies are provided to all individuals accessing DoD Component-owned or controlled DoD ISs.

n. Ensure that cybersecurity solutions do not unnecessarily restrict the use of assistive technology by individuals with disabilities or access to or use of information and data by individuals with disabilities in accordance with sections 791, 794, and 794d of Title 29, U.S.C. (Reference (bu)).

    o. Conduct vulnerability assessments, Blue Team vulnerability evaluations and intrusion assessments, cybersecurity inspections, and Red Team operations (using internal or external capabilities) to provide a systemic view of enclave and IS cybersecurity posture.

    p. Ensure that the cybersecurity testing and evaluation is conducted throughout the acquisition life cycle and integrated with interoperability and other functional testing, and that a cybersecurity representative participates in planning, execution, and reporting of integrated T&E activities as discussed in Enclosure 6 of Reference (av).

    q. Collect and report cybersecurity metrics, and ensure that an annual assessment of the DoD Component cybersecurity program is conducted as required by section 3545 of Reference (aa).

    r. Develop DoD IS contingency plans and conduct exercises to recover IS services following an emergency or IS disruption using guidance found in NIST SP 800-34 (Reference (bv)).

    s. Establish a physical security program to protect DoD IT from damage, loss, theft, or unauthorized physical access in accordance with DoD 5200.08-R (Reference (bw)).

    t. Ensure that all DoD ISs under their purview are registered in the DoD IT Portfolio Repository (DITPR) (at https://ditpr.dod.mil/) or the SIPRNET IT Registry (SITR) (at http://dodcio.osd.smil.mil/itregistry) in accordance with current DITPR and SITR guidance, or with the DoD Component SAP Central Office (SAPCO) for SAP ISs.

    u. Ensure that all DoD IT under their purview complies with applicable STIGs, security configuration guides, and SRGs with any exceptions documented and approved by the responsible AO.

    v. Establish a CD support element to coordinate CD activities with the UCDMO in accordance with DoD CIO Memorandum (Reference (bx)), and ensure transition from using CDSs on the UCDMO-managed CDS Sunset List to using CDSs on the UCDMO-managed CDS Baseline List.

    w. Ensure use of the DISA-provided CD Services as the preferred method of addressing CD requirements.

    x. Implement procedures issued by the DASD(DT&E) and DOT&E to ensure that cognizant T&E authorities for acquisition programs verify that adequate T&E support for cybersecurity requirements is planned, resourced, documented, and can be executed in a timely manner in accordance with References (bb), (bc), (bd), and (be).

    y. Ensure individual and organization accountability within organizations under their purview, including:

(1) Hold commanders, IS owners (ISOs), AOs, information system security managers (ISSMs) (formerly known as IA managers), information system security officers (ISSOs), program managers (PMs), project and application leads, supervisors, and system administrators responsible and accountable for the implementation of DoD security requirements in accordance with this instruction, References (v), (bo), (bp), (bs), and (bw), DoDM 5200.01, Volume 2 (Reference (by)), DoD 5220.22-R (Reference (bz)), and supplemental DoD Component guidance. Personnel filling positions with privileged access must be qualified and sign a Statement of Acceptance of Responsibilities in accordance with Reference (ba).

(2) Ensure that military and civilian personnel are considered for administrative or judicial sanctions if they knowingly, willfully, or negligently compromise, damage, or place at risk DoD information by not ensuring implementation of DoD security requirements in accordance with this instruction, other DoD 8500 series directives and instructions, DoD 5200 series instructions and publications, and supplemental DoD Component policies and procedures.

z. Ensure that requirements of CNSSP 300 (Reference (ca)), CNSSI 7000 (Reference (cb)), and other DIRNSA/CHNSS-issued guidance on compromising emanations (i.e., TEMPEST) are funded and implemented.

aa. Implement cybersecurity and cyberspace defense capabilities responsive to DoD requirements in accordance with Reference (bk) and (bl).

ab. Ensure that maintenance and disposal of information on DoD IT complies with the provisions of DoDD 5015.2 (Reference (cc)).

14. <u>CJCS</u>. In addition to the responsibilities in section 13 of this enclosure, the CJCS:

a. Provides advice and assessment on joint military requirements for cybersecurity assisted by the Joint Requirements Oversight Council in accordance with References (au) and (av).

b. Supports international cybersecurity and cyberspace defense activities of the DoD CIO.

c. Develops, coordinates, and promulgates cybersecurity policy, doctrine, and guidance for joint and combined operations consistent with this instruction, as required.

d. Appoints a PAO for DoD ISs and PIT systems governed by the Warfighting Mission Area as described in Reference (ac).

15. <u>COMMANDER, USSTRATCOM</u>. In addition to the responsibilities in section 13 of this enclosure, the Commander, USSTRATCOM:

a. Coordinates and directs DoD information networks operations and defense in accordance with the Unified Command Plan (Reference (cd)).

b. Ensures that Commander, USSTRATCOM orders addressing cybersecurity are consistent with the policy and guidance in this instruction and coordinated with the DoD CIO.

c. Chairs the DoD ISRMC and co-chairs the ESSG in accordance with References (aq) and (aj).

d. Oversees and ensures timely implementation of international cybersecurity and cyberspace defense agreements involving the geographic combatant commands.

e. Oversees DoD cybersecurity inspections as described in CJCSI 6510.01 (Reference (ce)) and operational risk assessments as described in NIST SP 800-30 (Reference (cf)) to maintain and determine compliance with security policy, procedures, and practices.

ENCLOSURE 3

PROCEDURES

1. INTRODUCTION

a. The purpose of the Defense cybersecurity program is to ensure that IT can be used in a way that allows mission owners and operators to have confidence in the confidentiality, integrity, and availability of IT and DoD information, and to make choices based on that confidence.

b. The Defense cybersecurity program supports DoD's vision of effective operations in cyberspace where:

(1) DoD missions and operations continue under any cyber situation or condition.

(2) The IT components of DoD weapons systems and other defense platforms perform as designed and adequately meet operational requirements.

(3) The DoD Information Enterprise collectively, consistently, and effectively acts in its own defense.

(4) DoD has ready access to its information and command and control channels, and its adversaries do not.

(5) The DoD Information Enterprise securely and seamlessly extends to mission partners.

c. In accordance with DoDD 5105.53 (Reference (cg)), the Director of Administration and Management is responsible for providing policy, oversight, direction, and control, including exercise of the authorities of the Secretary of Defense pursuant to chapter 159 of Reference (bh), for the management, operation, security, protection, safety, renovation, construction, and IT of the Pentagon Reservation and supported DoD facilities and space in the National Capital Region, including the Raven Rock Mountain Complex and alternate sites.

2. RISK MANAGEMENT

a. <u>Cybersecurity Risk Management</u>. Managing cybersecurity risks is a complex, multifaceted undertaking that requires the involvement of the entire organization, from senior leaders planning and managing DoD operations, to individuals developing, implementing, and operating the IT supporting those operations. Cybersecurity risk management is a subset of the overall risk management process for all DoD acquisitions as defined in Reference (av), which includes cost, performance, and schedule risk associated with the execution of all programs of record, and all other acquisitions of DoD. The risk assessment process extends to the logistics support of fielded equipment and the need to maintain the integrity of supply sources.

(1) DoD will use NIST SP 800-37 (Reference (ch)), as implemented by Reference (q), to address risk management, including authorization to operate (ATO), for all DoD ISs and PIT systems.

(2) DoD IS and PIT systems will transition to CNSSI 1253 (Reference (ci)), NIST SP 800-53 (Reference (cj)), and Reference (ch) in accordance with transition guidance provided in Reference (q).

b. <u>Integrated Organization-Wide Risk Management</u>. Risk management can be viewed as a holistic activity that is fully integrated into every aspect of the organization as described in Reference (o). Figure 1 illustrates a three-tiered approach to risk management that addresses risk-related concerns at the organization level, the mission and business process level, and the IS level.

<u>Figure 1</u>. Three-Tiered Approach to Risk Management

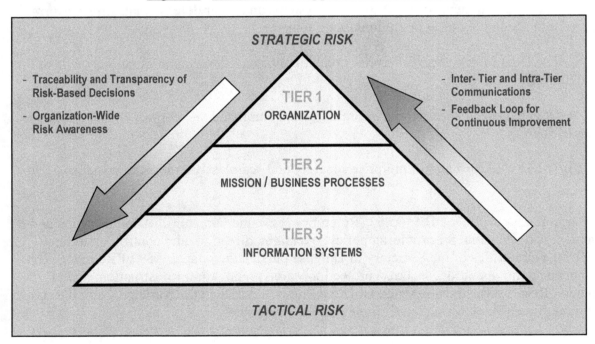

(1) Risk management at Tier 1 addresses risk from an organizational perspective. As part of the feedback loop, Tier 1 risk management is informed and influenced by risk decisions made in Tiers 2 and 3.

(a) A comprehensive IS security governance structure is established that provides assurance that IS security strategies are aligned with and support mission and business objectives, are consistent with applicable laws and regulations through adherence to policies and internal controls, and provide assignment of responsibility.

(b) The DoD ISRMC, comprising the four MA PAOs and other major DoD and IC stakeholders, provides the Tier 1 risk management governance for DoD.

(2) Tier 2 addresses risk from a mission and business process perspective and is guided by the risk decisions at Tier 1, and informed and influenced by risk decisions made in Tier 3.

(a) The activities at Tier 2 begin with the design, development, and implementation of the mission and business processes defined at Tier 1.

(b) The PAOs for each DoD MA provide the Tier 2 governance for their respective MAs.

(3) Tier 3 addresses risk from an IS and PIT system perspective and is guided by the risk decisions at Tiers 1 and 2.

(a) Though the need for specific protections is identified at Tiers 1 and 2, it is at Tier 3 where the information protections are applied to the system and its environment of operation for the benefit of successfully enabling mission and business success.

(b) Information protection requirements are satisfied by the selection and implementation of appropriate security controls in Reference (cj). Security controls are implemented at Tier 3 by common control providers, system managers (SMs), or PMs, and risk-based authorization decisions are granted by AOs.

c. Risk Management in the System Development Life Cycle

(1) Risk management tasks begin early in the system development life cycle and are important in shaping the security capabilities of the IS. If these tasks are not adequately performed during the initiation, development, and acquisition phases of the system development life cycle, the tasks will, by necessity, be undertaken later in the life cycle and will be more costly and time consuming to implement, and could negatively impact the performance of the IS.

(2) Cybersecurity risk management is planned for and documented in a cybersecurity strategy (formerly known as IA strategy) in accordance with References (at) and (av), and included in the PPP for all acquisition programs. Periodic reviews of the PPP and associated systems engineering documents should evaluate the status of cybersecurity solutions as part of the larger systems development.

(3) Risk management must continue during operations and sustainment. This may include the application of new or revised security controls prior to the integration of new IT services or products into an existing operational IS in order to maintain the security of the operational IS.

d. DoD ISRMC. The DoD ISRMC, supported by the DSAWG, is the DoD risk executive function as described in References (o) and (ch).

e. Risk Management Framework (RMF). DoD uses Reference (ch) as implemented by Reference (q), and is applicable to all DoD ISs and PIT systems. The RMF provides a disciplined and structured process that combines IS security and risk management activities into the system development life cycle and authorizes their use within DoD. The RMF has six steps: categorize system; select security controls; implement security controls; assess security controls; authorize system; and monitor security controls.

    f. <u>Risk Assessment</u>. Risk assessment is a key step in the organizational risk management process. Risk assessments will be performed in accordance with the process in Reference (cf) and as described on the Knowledge Service (KS) (i.e., recommending preferred risk assessment approaches and analysis approaches). In particular, all of the risk factors described in Reference (cf) must be used across components and agencies of the DoD to ensure reciprocity and ease of sharing risk information. The robustness of the risk assessments may be tailored to accommodate resource constraints and the availability of detailed risk factor information (e.g., threat data); however, any tailoring must be clearly explained in risk assessment reports to ensure that AOs understand to what degree they can rely on the results of the risk assessments.

    g. <u>Security Controls</u>. Security controls are expressed in a specified format (e.g., a control number, a control name, control text, and enhancement text).

    (1) All DoD IS and PIT systems will be categorized in accordance with Reference (ci) and will implement a corresponding set of security controls that are published in Reference (cj) regardless of whether they are National Security System (NSS) or non-NSS.

    (2) All security controls used by DoD are published in the security control catalog in Reference (cj), with supporting validation procedures in NIST 800-53A (Reference (ck)).

    (3) DoD-specific assignment values, implementation guidance, and validation procedures will be developed by the DoD CIO with direct support from NSA/CSS and DISA and input from the other DoD Components and will be published in the KS at https://diacap.iaportal.navy.mil.

    (4) The DoD CIO, with direct support from NSA/CSS and DISA, and input from the other DoD Components, works with NIST to ensure that the security control catalog remains up-to-date and continues to represent DoD needs.

    (5) Detailed guidance on DoD IS and PIT system categorization and security control selection is provided in Reference (q).

    h. <u>Cybersecurity Reciprocity</u>

    (1) Within DoD, reciprocity has been implemented as cybersecurity reciprocity to differentiate it from the application of reciprocity to other disciplines. Cybersecurity reciprocity reduces time and resources wasted on redundant test, assessment and documentation efforts.

    (2) Cybersecurity reciprocity is best achieved through transparency (i.e., making sufficient evidence regarding the security posture of an IS or PIT system available, so that an AO from another organization can use that evidence to make credible, risk-based decisions regarding the acceptance and use of that system or the information it processes, stores, or transmits). DoD

Components must share security authorization packages with affected information owners (IOs) or stewards and interconnected ISOs to support cybersecurity reciprocity. The reciprocal acceptance of DoD and other federal agency and department security authorizations will be implemented in accordance with the procedures in Reference (q).

3. <u>OPERATIONAL RESILIENCE</u>. Operational resilience requires three conditions to be met: information resources are trustworthy; missions are ready for information resources degradation or loss; and network operations have the means to prevail in the face of adverse events. Operational resilience must be achieved by:

   a. Using TSN requirements and best practices to protect mission-critical functions and components and manage risks to the integrity of critical information and communications technology in accordance with Reference (bm) for the sustainment of IT. This includes the use of criticality analysis, all-source threat informed acquisition, and engineering mitigations, and the authorities prescribed in section 806 of the Ike Skelton National Defense Authorization Act for Fiscal Year 2011(Reference (cl)). TSN processes and best practices must be applied early and across the system development life cycle, and be applied to system acquisitions and the purchase and integration of replacement IT as described in Reference (bm).

   b. Performing developmental T&E of cybersecurity in accordance with Reference (av) and OT&E in accordance with References (bc) and (bd), including the ability to detect and react to penetrations and exploitations and to protect and restore data and information, in order to inform acquisition and fielding decisions.

   c. Supporting acquisition program protection by:

      (1) Ensuring cybersecurity is a key element of program protection planning activities that manage risks to advance technology and mission-critical system functionality from foreign collection due to design vulnerability or supply chain exploit insertion, and battlefield loss throughout the system life cycle.

      (2) Having mission criteria for identifying critical components and critical program information as established in References (bm) and (ay).

   d. Planning for mission continuation in the face of degraded or unavailable information resources in accordance with DoDD 3020.26 (Reference (cm)), and integrating those plans and priorities into the DoD Information Enterprise.

   e. Exercising under realistic cyber conditions and testing procedures and tactics for work-arounds and fall-backs in the face of hostility in accordance with Secretary of Defense Memorandum (Reference (cn)). This includes:

      (1) Conducting periodic exercises or evaluations of the ability to operate during loss of all information resources and connectivity.

(2) Being able to allocate information resources dynamically as needed to sustain mission operations while addressing cyber failures, no matter the cause.

(3) Being able to restore information resources rapidly to a trusted state while maintaining support to ongoing missions.

f. Preserving the trust in the security of DoD information during transmission.

(1) Transmission of DoD information must be protected through the communications security (COMSEC) measures and procedures established in DoDI 8523.01 (Reference (co)) and security controls that support transmission security (TRANSEC) in Reference (cj).

(2) COMSEC monitoring and cybersecurity readiness testing will be conducted in accordance with Reference (bn).

(3) Compromising emanations (i.e., TEMPEST) countermeasures must be applied in accordance with policy in Reference (ca), guidance in Reference (cb), and other TEMPEST guidance as issued by the DIRNSA/CHCSS.

g. Using automation whenever possible in support of cybersecurity objectives including, but not limited to, secure configuration management, continuous monitoring, active cyber defense, and incident reporting and situational awareness.

4. INTEGRATION AND INTEROPERABILITY

a. Net-Centric Operations. A net-centric model provides people, services, and platforms the ability to discover one another and connect to form new capabilities or teams without being constrained by geographic, organizational, or technical barriers. The net-centric model allows people, services, and platforms to work together to achieve shared ends. To be net-centric, cybersecurity will be designed, organized, and managed such that it can work together in any combination that events demand and maintain an expected level of readiness so that all required cybersecurity assets can be brought to bear in a rapid and flexible manner to meet new or changing mission needs.

b. Integration. Cybersecurity must be fully integrated into system life cycles so that it will be a visible element of organizational, joint, and DoD Component architectures, capability identification and development processes, integrated testing, information technology portfolios, acquisition, operational readiness assessments, supply chain risk management, SSE, and operations and maintenance activities.

c. Interoperability

(1) Cybersecurity products (e.g., firewalls, file integrity checkers, virus scanners, intrusion detection systems, anti-malware software) should operate in a net-centric manner to enhance the exchange of data and shared security policies.

(2) Semantic, technical, and policy interoperability will be used to integrate disparate cybersecurity products into a net-centric enterprise that can work together to create new intelligence and make and implement decisions at network speed.

(3) Semantic, technical, and policy interoperability support products are designed to provide security for communications between different IT systems. Interoperable communications must be consistent with approved cryptographic design and current system implementation standards. The objective is to ensure the seamless and secure exchange of classified or sensitive information that is critical to the success of DoD mission goals and objectives.

d. <u>Standards-Based Approach</u>. The DoD cybersecurity and cyberspace defense data strategy will enable semantic, technical, and policy interoperability through a standards-based approach that has been refined by many in industry, academia, and government. It is an information-oriented approach (see for example the security content automation protocol (SCAP) discussion in NIST SP 800-126 (Reference (cp)).

e. <u>DoD Architecture Principles</u>. Interoperability and effective management of security content will be achieved through adherence to DoD cybersecurity architectures as issued. All DoD Components must commit to these architectures to facilitate sharing of information necessary to achieve mission success while managing the risk inherent in interconnecting systems.

f. <u>Knowledge Repositories</u>. These contain a broad collection of best practices, benchmarks, standards, templates, checklists, tools, guidelines, rules, principles, and the like. Examples include the National Vulnerability Database (http://nvd.nist.gov/), the Open Vulnerability and Assessment Language Repository (http://oval.mitre.org/repository), and the DoD's KS as defined in Reference (q). In many respects, knowledge repositories serve as the cybersecurity and cyberspace defense community "memory" and they enable policy or process interoperability and should be used to share information and answer questions.

5. <u>CYBERSPACE DEFENSE</u>. Cyberspace defense uses architectures, cybersecurity, intelligence, counterintelligence (CI), other security programs, LE, and other military capabilities to harden the DoD Information Enterprise to be more resistant to penetration and disruption; to strengthen the U.S. ability to respond to unauthorized activity and defend DoD information and networks against sophisticated and agile cyber threats; and to recover quickly from cyber incidents.

a. <u>Defense of DoD IT</u>. Defense of DoD IT and information networks is under the direction of the Commander, USSTRATCOM, in accordance with Reference (cd) and is conducted as described in Commander, USSTRATCOM, orders or other directives such as alerts and bulletins, Reference (bl), and DoD Manual O-8530.01 (Reference (cq)). Cyberspace defense is integrated with other elements of network operations as described in DoDI 8410.02 (Reference (cr)).

b. <u>Continuous Monitoring Capability</u>. DoD will establish and maintain a continuous monitoring capability that provides cohesive collection, transmission, storage, aggregation, and presentation of data that conveys current operational status to affected DoD stakeholders. DoD Components will achieve cohesion through the use of a common continuous monitoring framework, lexicon, and workflow as specified in NIST SP 800-137 (Reference (cs)).

c. <u>Penetration and Exploitation Testing</u>. Evaluation of cybersecurity during an acquisition T&E event must include independent threat representative penetration and exploitation testing and evaluation of the complete system cyberspace defenses including the controls and protection provided by computer network defense service providers. Penetration and exploitation testing must be planned and resourced as part of the DT&E and OT&E via the appropriate program test documentation.

d. <u>Cyber Defense Personnel</u>. Cyber defense personnel operating on or in DoD IS will be identified using identity authentication methods in DoDI 8520.03 (Reference (ct)).

e. <u>LE and CI (LE/CI)</u>

(1) The DoD Cyber Crime Center, as described in DoDD 5505.13 (Reference (cu)), provides digital and multimedia forensics and specialized cyber investigative training and services. In this role it coordinates and facilitates relationships across LE, intelligence, and homeland security communities.

(2) DoD component LE/CI agencies deploy capabilities on DoD networks with the intent to identify and investigate the human element posing a threat to DoD IT and DoD information. Cybersecurity will be used in support of countering espionage, international terrorism, and the CI insider threat in accordance with DoDI 5240.26 (Reference (cv)).

(3) DoD network administrators will accommodate all applicable legitimate and lawful deployment of LE/CI tools and solutions. DoD LE/CI organizations in turn will make all reasonable attempts to coordinate the implementation of LE/CI solutions with their respective AO in a manner consistent with service-level change control processes in order to avoid any disruption to mission critical operational tempo.

f. <u>Insider Threat</u>. Insider threats must be addressed in accordance with policy and procedures published by the USD(P).

6. <u>PERFORMANCE</u>

a. Organizations will implement processes and procedures to accommodate three conditions necessary to realize effective cybersecurity that is consistently implemented across DoD:

(1) <u>Organization Direction</u>. This includes organizational mechanisms for establishing and communicating priorities and objectives, principles, policies, standards, and performance

measures.

    (2) <u>A Culture of Accountability</u>. This includes aligning internal processes, maintaining accountability, and informing, making, and following through on decisions with implications for cyberspace protection and defense.

    (3) <u>Insight and Oversight</u>. This includes measuring, reviewing, verifying, monitoring, facilitating, and remediating to ensure coordinated and consistent cybersecurity implementation and reporting across all organizations without impeding local missions.

    b. In addition to the structures that facilitate DoD's major decision processes (e.g., the Joint Chiefs of Staff Joint Capabilities Integration and Development System described in CJCSI 3170.01 (Reference (cw)), DoDD 7045.14 (Reference (cx)), Reference (au)) cybersecurity performance is facilitated by the DoD CIO Executive Board in accordance with the DoD CIO Memorandum (Reference (cy)) and its supporting governance bodies (e.g., IA Senior Leadership forum, DoD ISRMC).

    c. Strategic cybersecurity metrics will be defined, collected, and reported by the DoD CIO in partnership with the DoD Components. DoD CIO will develop and issue guidance regarding how cybersecurity metrics are determined, established, defined, collected, and reported.

7. <u>DoD INFORMATION</u>

    a. The DoD Information Security Program is described in DoDI 5200.01 (Reference (cz)). All classified information and CUI must be protected in accordance with References (bs), (by), (bo), and (bp).

    b. DoD's information sharing policies and procedures are defined in DoDD 8320.02 (Reference (da)) and DoD 8320.02-G (Reference (db)). Information sharing actions and activities will be aligned with the DoD Information Sharing Operational Strategy and Guidance (see www.dodcio.defense.gov). A security clearance held is an attribute of any identified DoD person, and that attribute should be discovered and considered when a decision is made to share classified information. If the information intended to be shared is not classified, then other attributes associated with the identity of the sharing recipient may need to be discovered before the sharing is executed.

    c. The Defense cybersecurity program provides the mechanisms to measure, monitor, and enforce information security and sharing policies and procedures as they relate to information in an electronic form, primarily through the implementation of security controls.

    d. Information systems must protect classified information and CUI from unauthorized access by requiring authentication in accordance with Reference (ct) prior to making an access decision.

e. All unclassified DoD information that has not been cleared for public release in accordance with DoDD 5230.09 (Reference (dc)) and that is in the possession or control of non-DoD entities on non-DoD ISs must be protected in accordance with DoDI 8582.01 (Reference (dd)).

f. Classified information and export controlled unclassified information released or disclosed to industry in connection with contracts under the National Industrial Security Program must be protected in accordance with Reference (bj).

g. Spillage of classified information onto an unclassified IS, of higher-level classified information onto a lower level classified IS, or of classified information onto an IS not authorized to the appropriate level must be handled in accordance with Reference (bo).

h. To enable automated sharing and protection, all DoD information must include marking and metadata as required by References (bp), (bs) and (da), and that information must be in the format specified in References (bp) and (by).

i. DoD IT that processes or stores PII or protected health information must comply with Reference (bq), DoDI 5400.16 (Reference (de)), and DoD 8580.02-R (Reference (df)).

j. In accordance with Reference (de), a privacy impact assessment (PIA) is required for DoD ISs that collect, maintain, use, or disseminate PII about members of the public, federal personnel, contractors, or foreign nationals (FNs) employed at U.S. military facilities internationally.

k. All non-DoD entities that process unclassified DoD information on non-DoD ISs, to the extent provided by the applicable contract, grant, or other legal agreement or understanding with DoD, must comply with applicable Defense Federal Acquisition Regulation Supplements and will comply with Reference (dd), and, if a cleared contractor, with Reference (bj).

l. Unclassified DoD information in the possession of the DIB will be protected by conducting DIB cybersecurity as established in Reference (ad), and cleared contractor facilities will be protected in accordance with Reference (bj).

m. Cryptography required to protect DoD information will be implemented in accordance with Reference (bi).

n. DoD information proposed or projected for publication on public Internet media (e.g., website, blog, social media) must be reviewed and approved for public dissemination in accordance with Reference (dc), DoD Manual 5205.02 (Reference (dg)), and DoDI 8550.01 (Reference (dh)).

8. IDENTITY ASSURANCE

a. Identity assurance ensures strong identification and authentication, and eliminates anonymity in DoD ISs so that entities' access and access behavior are visible, traceable, and enable continuous monitoring for LE and cybersecurity. Person and non-person entity identity policies, standards, information, infrastructure, issuance, and revocation processes and procedures that bind the physical and digital representations of entities will incorporate measures to ensure the integrity, authenticity, security, privacy, and availability of authoritative identity information across the full spectrum of DoD mission environments and operations.

(1) DoD ISs will use only DoD-approved identity credentials to authenticate entities requesting access to or within the Defense information environment. This requirement extends to all mission partners using DoD ISs.

(2) The identification of entities accessing DoD ISs must be recorded in order to deny anonymity and deter abuse of authorized IS access. DoD will implement capabilities to record, track, and monitor specific entity access to networks, applications, and web servers.

b. DoD IS will employ identity assurance procedures that are aligned with the DoD Identity Management Strategic Plan and the Identity Assurance Implementation Guidance and Roadmap to the extent practical.

c. Information and infrastructure that support identity reliant functions, processes, and procedures used in support of DoD operations, including but not limited to identity credentialing, will incorporate measures to ensure the confidentiality, integrity, authenticity, and availability of identity data or identity credentials.

d. Identity assurance policies and procedures regarding identity authentication for ISs are in Reference (ct).

9. INFORMATION TECHNOLOGY

a. IT. Cybersecurity applies to all IT that receives, processes, stores, displays, or transmits DoD information, as shown in Figure 2.

Figure 2. DoD Information Technology

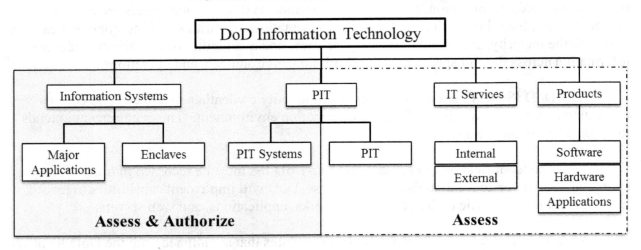

(1) Information Systems. Cybersecurity requirements must be identified and included in the design, development, acquisition, installation, operation, upgrade, or replacement of all DoD ISs in accordance with section 3544 of Reference (aa), References (q) and (r), section 2224 of Reference (bh), this instruction, and other cybersecurity-related DoD guidance, as issued.

(a) DoD ISs are typically organized in one of two forms:

1. Enclave

a. Enclaves provide standard cybersecurity, such as boundary defense, incident detection and response, and key management, and also deliver common applications, such as office automation and electronic mail. Enclaves may be specific to an organization or a mission, and the computing environments may be organized by physical proximity or by function independent of location. Examples of enclaves include local area networks and the applications they host, backbone networks, and data processing centers.

b. Enclaves always assume the highest security category of the ISs that they host, and derive their security needs from those systems. See Reference (ch) for a discussion of IS boundaries and the application of security controls.

2. Major Application (Formerly Automated Information System Application)

a. Certain applications, because of the information in them, require special management oversight due to the risk and magnitude of the harm resulting from the loss, misuse, or unauthorized access to or modification of the information in the application and should be treated as major applications. A major application may be a single software application (e.g., integrated consumable items support); multiple software applications that are related to a single mission (e.g., payroll or personnel); or a combination of software and hardware performing a specific support function across a range of missions (e.g., Global Command and Control System, Defense Enrollment Eligibility Reporting System).

<u>b</u>. Major applications include any application that is a product or deliverable of an Acquisition Category I through III program as defined in Enclosure 3 of Reference (av). When operationally feasible all new major applications will be hosted in a Defense Enterprise Computing Center.

<u>c</u>. All applications, regardless of whether they rise to the level of major application or not, require an appropriate level of protection. Adequate security for other than major applications may be provided by security of the environment in which they operate.

<u>d</u>. When possible, capabilities should be developed as applications hosted in existing authorized computing environments (i.e., enclaves) rather than designated as major applications requiring new and separate authorizations.

<u>e</u>. DoD Component CIOs will resolve disputes regarding whether an application rises to the level of a major application.

(b) <u>DoD IS Registration</u>. All DoD ISs will be registered in the DITPR (at https://ditpr.dod.mil/) or the SITR (at http://dodcio.osd.smil.mil/itregistry) in accordance with current DITPR and SITR guidance, or with the DoD Component SAPCO for SAP ISs. New DoD ISs should be entered into the DITPR or SITR at the beginning of the system development life cycle.

(c) <u>Stand-Alone Systems</u>. DoD ISs and PIT systems that are stand-alone must be authorized to operate, but assigned security control sets may be tailored as appropriate with the approval of the AO (e.g., network-related controls may be eliminated).

(d) <u>Notice and Consent Banners</u>. Standard mandatory notice and consent banners must be displayed at logon to all ISs and standard mandatory notice and consent provisions will be included in all DoD IS user agreements in accordance with applicable security controls and DoD implementation procedures in the KS. Official DoD standard notice and consent language will be posted on the KS with copies posted to the IASE.

(2) <u>PIT</u>

(a) All PIT has cybersecurity considerations. The Defense cybersecurity program only addresses the protection of the IT included in the platform. See Reference (q) for PIT cybersecurity requirements.

(b) Examples of platforms that may include PIT are: weapons systems, training simulators, diagnostic test and maintenance equipment, calibration equipment, equipment used in the research and development of weapons systems, medical devices and health information technologies, vehicles and alternative fueled vehicles (e.g., electric, bio-fuel, Liquid Natural Gas that contain car-computers), buildings and their associated control systems (building automation systems or building management systems, energy management system, fire and life safety, physical security, elevators, etc.), utility distribution systems (such as electric, water, waste water, natural gas and steam), telecommunications systems designed specifically for industrial control systems including supervisory control and data acquisition, direct digital control, programmable logic controllers, other control devices and advanced metering or sub-metering, including associated data transport mechanisms (e.g., data links, dedicated networks).

(c) Cybersecurity requirements must be identified, tailored appropriately, and included in the acquisition, design, development, developmental and operational testing and evaluation, integration, implementation, operation, upgrade, or replacement of all DoD PIT in accordance with References (bm) and (ay), this instruction, and other cybersecurity-related DoD guidance, as issued.

(d) Owners of special purpose systems (i.e., platforms), in consultation with an AO, may determine that a collection of PIT rises to the level of a PIT system.

<u>1</u>.   PIT systems are analogous to enclaves but are dedicated only to the platforms they support. PIT systems must be designated as such by the responsible OSD or DoD Component heads or their delegates and authorized by an AO specifically appointed to authorize PIT systems.

<u>2</u>. All DoD PIT systems will be categorized as defined in Reference (ci) and authorized in accordance with Reference (q).

<u>3</u>. Although other federal departments and agencies may treat PIT systems as a type of IS, DoD platforms supporting certain DoD missions have unique operational and security needs. Due to the specialized purpose of their application, PIT systems require uniquely tailored security control sets and control validation procedures and require security control assessors and AOs with specialized qualifications.

<u>4</u>. Interconnections between PIT systems and other PIT systems or DoD ISs must be protected either by implementation of security controls on the PIT system or the DoD IS.

<u>5</u>. For PIT systems that are stand-alone, assigned security control sets may be tailored as appropriate with the approval of the AO (e.g., network-related controls may be eliminated).

<u>6</u>. PIT systems must be registered at the DoD Component level.

(3) <u>IT Service</u>. An IT service is a form of a DoD internet service as described in Reference (dh). It consists of IT capabilities that are provided according to a formal agreement between DoD entities or between DoD and an entity external to DoD. Capabilities may include, for example, information processing, storage, or transmission.

(a) An IT service is provided from outside the authorization boundary of the organizational IS using the IT service and the using organization typically has no direct control over the application of required security controls or the assessment of security control effectiveness.

(b) IT services are net-centric and may be provided over service oriented or cloud computing architectures and may be Internet-based.

(c) An internal IT service is implemented within DoD. The DoD entity providing the service is responsible for the application of appropriate security controls and for ensuring that ISs supporting service delivery are assessed and authorized in accordance with Reference (q). Service-level agreements (SLAs) will be executed for internal services.

(d) An external IT service is implemented outside DoD. The DoD entity using the external service will:

<u>1</u>. Ensure that interagency agreements or government statements of work for external services incorporate requirements in accordance with this instruction. Requirements for external services must include the application of appropriate security controls to the IT supporting the external service delivery in accordance with Reference (q). Requests for proposals will include sufficient information on which to evaluate each offeror's proposed approach to satisfying the security control requirements.

<u>2</u>. Ensure that processes, roles, and responsibilities are established between program management office and network operations entities for continued assessment.

<u>3</u>. Ensure that all security relevant and operational status changes are reported through the organization's network operations chain of command to the Commander, USSTRATCOM.

<u>4</u>. DoD enterprise-level agreements for services should be used when possible.

(4) <u>IT Product</u>

(a) Unified capability products will receive unified capability certification for cybersecurity in accordance with Reference (ao).

(b) Products that protect classified information must comply with Reference (bg).

(c) Products must meet security configuration guidance in accordance with Chapter 113 of Reference (s) and comply with the connection approval process established in Reference (am).

(d) Products will comply with the requirements of Reference (bm), as applicable.

b. <u>IT Considerations</u>. These are general considerations that apply to IT.

(1) All acquisitions of DoD IS will comply with Reference (at) and USD(AT&L) Memorandum (Reference (di)).

(2) SMs and PMs must use TSN tools, techniques, and practices, including the use of all-source threat assessments to inform acquisition and engineering mitigation decisions, for all IT when required in accordance with Reference (bm). During sustainment, TSN practices will be applied prior to integrating IT into operational IS.

(3) Cybersecurity will be implemented in all system and service acquisitions at levels appropriate to the system characteristics and requirements throughout the entire life cycle of the acquisition in accordance with Reference (q).

(4) All acquisitions of qualifying IT must have an adequate and appropriate cybersecurity strategy that will be reviewed prior to acquisition milestone decisions and acquisition contract awards in accordance with References (at), (av), and Section 811 of Public Law 106-398 (Reference (dj)) and must plan for developmental test oversight by DASD(DT&E) and operational test oversight by DOT&E.

(5) Each mobile code technology used in DoD information systems must undergo a risk assessment, be assigned to a mobile code risk category, and have its use regulated based on its potential to cause damage to DoD operations and interests if used maliciously.

(6) Ports, protocols, and services will be managed in accordance with Reference (an).

(7) DoD use of space systems will follow cybersecurity policy established in DoDI 8581.01 (Reference (dk)).

(8) Disposal and destruction of classified hard drives, electronic media, processing equipment components, and the like will be accomplished in accordance with Reference (bo), CNSSI 4004.1 (Reference (dl)), and applicable security controls.

(9) Disposal of unclassified electronic media will be accomplished in accordance with the guidelines provided in NIST SP 800-88 (Reference (dm)) and applicable security controls.

(10) Cryptographic products used to protect IT and the information that resides in the IT will be acquired and implemented in accordance with Reference (bi).

(11) All IA products and IA-enabled products that require use of the product's IA capabilities will comply with the evaluation and validation requirements of Reference (bg).

(12) All IT will be assigned to and governed by a DoD Component cybersecurity program.

(13) IT below the system level (i.e., IT services and products) will be security configured and reviewed by the cognizant ISSM (under the direction of the AO) for acceptance and connection into an authorized computing environment (i.e., an IS enclave with an ATO).

(14) Cybersecurity must be consistent with enterprise architecture principles and guidelines within the DoD Architecture Framework (Reference (dn)) and DoD cybersecurity architectures developed or approved by the DoD CIO.

(15) Connections to the DISN must comply with connection approval procedures and processes as established in Reference (am).

(16) The ESSG will oversee development and acquisition of enterprise solutions for use throughout DoD that support cybersecurity objectives in accordance with Reference (aj).

(17) All persons entrusted with the management of DoD IT will be responsible for proper use, care, physical protection, and disposal or disposition in accordance with DoDI 5000.64 (Reference (do)), DoDI 2030.02 (Reference (dp)) and, when appropriate, Reference (bo).

(18) In addition to complying with the provisions of DoDI 1035.01 (Reference (dq)):

(a) Telework solutions involving the use of DoD-owned, government-furnished equipment for remote access to unclassified DoD networks will comply with the requirements of applicable security controls defined in Reference (cj).

(b) Telework solutions involving the use of non-government furnished equipment (i.e., any computer or other telework device not furnished by DoD) for remote access to unclassified DoD networks will be developed by the DoD Components desiring the capability based on the guidance provided in NIST SP 800-114 (Reference (dr)) and evaluated and approved by the DoD CIO on a case-by-case basis.

(19) Basic input and output systems (BIOSs) will be managed in accordance with Section 3.2 of SP 800-147 (Reference (ds)). Specifications for personal computer client systems must include the requirement for BIOS protections compliant with Section 3.1 of Reference (ds).

(20) In anticipation of emerging trusted platform module (TPM) product capabilities, as well as requirements for device identification, authentication, encryption, measurement, and device integrity, DoD Components will ensure new computer assets (e.g., server, desktop, laptop, thin client, tablet, smartphone, personal digital assistant, mobile phone) procured to support DoD will include a TPM version 1.2 or higher where required by DISA STIGs and where such technology is available.

(a) Vendor TPMs must be in conformance with Trusted Computing Group standards (www.trustedcomputinggroup.org/groups/tpm) and must be approved by the procuring DoD Component. The TPM must be turned on and ready for provisioning when the computer asset is received from the vendor. Written justification must be provided to the responsible AO if assets are procured without TPM technology in cases where it is available.

(b) DIRNSA will identify use cases and implementation standards and plans for DoD to leverage TPM functionality fully to enhance IT device security, including platform integrity verification (BIOS firmware and operating system software), platform identification and authentication, and enhanced encryption (hardware based key generation and certificate and key storage).

(21) DoD IT must comply with SCAP standards established in Reference (cp). STIGs developed by DISA will use SCAP standards.

(22) All use of Internet-based capabilities will comply with References (bp), (dc), (dg), and (dh).

(23) As the NIST and CNSS publications change, the impact of those changes will be incorporated into the KS.

(24) All DoD IT that is designated as an NSS must comply with CNSS policy issuances.

10. <u>CYBERSECURITY WORKFORCE</u>

a. The DoD IA Workforce Improvement Program develops and maintains a trained and qualified cybersecurity workforce by providing a continuum of learning from basic literacy to advanced skills, recruiting and retaining highly qualified professionals, and keeping workforce capabilities current in the face of constant change as described in References (w) and (ba).

b. All cybersecurity personnel must be assigned in writing to identified cybersecurity positions, and trained and qualified in accordance with References (w) and (ba).

c. All authorized users of DoD IS must receive initial cybersecurity awareness orientation as a condition of access and, thereafter, participate in both DoD's and their Component's enterprise cybersecurity awareness program.

d. Cybersecurity functions, as defined in Reference (ba), that may be performed by non-U.S. citizens, non-DoD personnel, contractors, or non-U.S. service providers will be so identified.

e. All cybersecurity positions will be assigned a position designation using the criteria found in References (v) and (bs) and will meet the associated suitability and fitness requirements. The position designation will be documented in the DCPDS. Non-U.S. citizens may not serve as ISSMs, as ISSOs, in supervisory cybersecurity positions, or be responsible for PKI certificate issuance. Non-U.S. citizens may serve as system administrators and perform maintenance on cybersecurity enabled products provided they are under the immediate supervision of a U.S. citizen and meet the investigative requirements of Reference (v).

11. <u>MISSION PARTNERS</u>

a. Integral to the success of the Defense cybersecurity program is the promotion of systems and communications interoperability and advancement of operational cybersecurity and cyberspace defense relationships with all mission partners at both the unclassified and classified levels; integration of cybersecurity and cyberspace defense activities with mission partner critical infrastructure protection initiatives; and creating cybersecurity and cyberspace defense training and exercise opportunities to build mission partner operational capacity, improve global cyber situational awareness, and develop a collective global cybersecurity and cyberspace defense workforce. This will be accomplished through the planning, negotiation, and implementation of cybersecurity and cyberspace defense agreements with mission partners.

b. DoD will operate a PKI for use by foreign national (FN) mission partners to communicate with Combatant Commands that will enable use of digital signature, encryption, and PKI-based authentication and be implemented and operated in accordance with DoD Coalition Public Key Infrastructure, X.509 Certificate Policy (Reference (dt)).

c. Foreign exchange personnel and representatives of foreign nations, coalitions or international organizations may be authorized access to DoD ISs containing classified or sensitive information only if these conditions are met:

(1) Access to DoD ISs is authorized only by the DoD Component head in accordance with DoD, Department of State, and ODNI disclosure guidance, as applicable.

(2) Mechanisms are in place to limit access strictly to information that has been cleared for release to the represented foreign nation, coalition, or international organization (e.g., North Atlantic Treaty Organization) in accordance with Reference (ab) for classified military information, and other policy guidance for unclassified information such as References (bp), (dp), DoDD 5230.20E (Reference (du)), and DoDI 5230.27 (Reference (dv)).

d. Capabilities built to support cybersecurity objectives that are shared with mission partners will be governed through integrated decision structures and processes described in this instruction, must have formal agreements (e.g., a memorandum of agreement, memorandum of understanding, SLAs, contracts, grants, or other legal agreements or understandings) that incorporate considerations for DoD risks, be in accordance with Reference (am), and will be consistent with applicable guidance contained in References (ab), (bo), (bp), (bu), (bs), (by), and DoDI 2040.02 (Reference (dw)).

e. Information systems jointly developed by DoD and mission partners are considered DoD-partnered systems. The cybersecurity risk management considerations for DoD-partnered systems are provided in Reference (q).

f. Agreements with international partners to engage in cooperative international cybersecurity activities must be formally negotiated and concluded in accordance with Reference (ag), and any associated classified military information will be released only in accordance with Reference (ab).

g. The release of cryptographic national security systems technical security material, information, and techniques to foreign governments or international organizations must be approved by the CNSS in accordance with Reference (ak).

12. <u>DoD SISO</u>. On behalf of the DoD CIO, the DoD SISO:

    a. Directs and coordinates the Defense cybersecurity program and, as delegated, carries out the DoD CIO's responsibilities pursuant to section 3544 of Reference (aa).

    b. Serves as the DoD CIO's primary liaison to DoD AOs, ISOs, and ISSOs.

    c. Advises, informs, and supports DoD PAOs and their representatives.

    d. Ensures that DoD IT is assigned to and governed by a DoD Component cybersecurity program.

    e. Maintains liaison with DNI CIO to ensure continuous coordination of DoD and IC cybersecurity activities and programs.

    f. Maintains liaison with NIST to ensure continuous coordination and collaboration on NIST cybersecurity-related issuances.

    g. Provides guidance and oversight in the development, submission, and execution of the DoD cybersecurity program budget and advocates for DoD-wide cybersecurity solutions throughout the planning, programming, budget, and execution process.

    h. Develops guidance regarding how cybersecurity metrics are determined, established, defined, collected, and reported.

    i. Collects and reports cybersecurity metrics in coordination with the DoD Component heads as required by section 3545 of Reference (aa).

    j. Coordinates with USD(AT&L) to integrate cybersecurity concepts into the DoD acquisition process by:

        (1) Supporting the USD(AT&L) in ensuring the DoD acquisition process incorporates cybersecurity planning, implementation, and testing consistent with References (p), section 3544 of (aa), (q), (at), (av), and this instruction.

        (2) Supporting the USD(AT&L) in its acquisition oversight of major defense acquisition programs, major automated ISs, or other programs of special interest that are, or include, IT, by:

            (a) Providing subject matter experts to participate in AT&L oversight of system engineering technical reviews and the review of system engineering artifacts to ensure that cybersecurity requirements are incorporated early and that the implementation of those requirements is maturing across the acquisition life cycle.

            (b) Informing USD(AT&L) of acquisition program risk related to a failure to address cybersecurity requirements in accordance with this policy.

k. Coordinates with the DOT&E to ensure cybersecurity testing and evaluation is integrated into the DoD acquisition process in accordance with References (bc), (bd), and other DOT&E policies and guidance.

l. Coordinates with USD(P) to ensure cybersecurity policies related to disclosure of classified military information to foreign governments and international organizations is in accordance with Reference (af) and (ab).

m. Provides recommended updates and additions to NIST for security controls that are published in Reference (cj) and for supporting validation procedures published in Reference (ck) with direct support from NSA/CSS and DISA, and input from the other DoD Components.

n. Provides recommended updates and additions to the security control baselines and overlays that are published in Reference (ci) and used by DoD with direct support from NSA/CSS and DISA, and input from the other DoD Components.

o. Develops DoD-specific assignment values, implementation guidance, and validation procedures for Reference (cj) security controls and publishes them in the KS at https://diacap.iaportal.navy.mil with direct support from NSA/CSS and DISA, and input from the other DoD Components.

p. Ensures that organization-wide solutions that support cybersecurity objectives acquired and developed via the ESSG process in accordance with Reference (aj) are consistent with DoD architecture, policy, and guidance developed by the DoD CIO to ensure solutions acquired or developed meet organizational requirements.

q. Manages international cybersecurity and cyberspace defense activities and represents DoD in carrying out assigned international cybersecurity and cyberspace defense responsibilities and functions through the International Cybersecurity Program.

r. Manages and executes DoD DIB Cybersecurity and IA Program activities in accordance with Reference (ad).

13. <u>DoD COMPONENT CIOs</u>. DoD Component CIOs:

a. On behalf of the respective DoD Component heads, develop, implement, maintain, and enforce a DoD Component cybersecurity program that is consistent with the strategy and direction of the DoD SISO and the Defense cybersecurity program, and compliant with this instruction.

b. Appoint DoD Component SISOs to direct and coordinate their DoD Component cybersecurity program.

c. When code signing certificates are used to establish provenance of software code, implement a process to designate individuals authorized to receive code-signing certificates and ensure that such designations are kept to a minimum consistent with operational requirements.

d. Partner with DoD Component Acquisition Executives to ensure that all IT is acquired in accordance with DoD cybersecurity policy and that program risk relating to the development of cybersecurity requirements is assessed, communicated to the Milestone Decision Authority and managed early in the system development life cycle.

14. DoD RISK EXECUTIVE FUNCTION. The risk executive function, as described in Reference (ch), is performed by the DoD ISRMC. The DoD risk executive:

a. Ensures risk-related considerations for individual ISs and PIT systems, including authorization decisions, are viewed from a DoD-wide perspective with regard to the overall strategic goals and objectives of DoD in carrying out its missions and business functions.

b. Ensures that management of IT-related security risks is consistent across DoD, reflects organizational risk tolerance, and is considered along with other organizational risk in order to ensure mission or business success.

15. PAO. PAOs:

a. Oversee and establish guidance for the strategic implementation of cybersecurity and risk management within their MAs.

b. Appoint flag-level (e.g., general officer, senior executive) PAO representatives to, and to oversee, the DoD ISRMC.

c. Assist the DoD CIO and DoD SISO in assessing the effectiveness of DoD cybersecurity.

16. AO. AOs:

a. Ensure that:

(1) For DoD ISs and PIT systems under their purview, cybersecurity-related positions are identified in their organization's manpower structure in accordance with References (w), (ba), and DoDI 1100.22 (Reference (dx)).

(2) Appointees to cybersecurity-related positions are given a written statement of cybersecurity responsibilities.

(3) ISSMs meet all requirements specified in Reference (v).

b. Render authorization decisions for DoD ISs and PIT systems under their purview in accordance with Reference (q).

c. Establish guidance for and oversee IS-level risk management activities consistent with Commander, USSTRATCOM, and DoD Component guidance and direction.

d. Must be U.S. citizens and DoD officials with the authority to assume responsibility formally for operating DoD ISs or PIT systems at an acceptable level of risk to organizational operations (including mission, functions, image, or reputation), organizational assets, individuals, other organizations, and the Nation.

17. <u>ISOs of DoD IT</u>. ISOs of DoD IT:

a. Plan and budget for security control implementation, assessment, and sustainment throughout the system life cycle, including timely and effective configuration and vulnerability management.

b. Ensure that SSE is used to design, develop, implement, modify, and test and evaluate the system architecture in compliance with the cybersecurity component of the DoD Enterprise Architecture (as described in Reference (r)) and to make maximum use of enterprise cybersecurity.

c. Ensure authorized users and support personnel receive appropriate cybersecurity training.

d. Coordinate with the DoD Component TSN focal point to ensure that TSN best practices, processes, techniques, and procurement tools are applied prior to the acquisition of IT or the integration of IT into ISs when required in compliance with Reference (bm).

18. <u>ISSM</u>. ISSMs:

a. Develop and maintain an organizational or system-level cybersecurity program that includes cybersecurity architecture, requirements, objectives and policies, cybersecurity personnel, and cybersecurity processes and procedures.

b. Ensure that IOs and stewards associated with DoD information received, processed, stored, displayed, or transmitted on each DoD IS and PIT system are identified in order to establish accountability, access approvals, and special handling requirements.

c. Maintain a repository for all organizational or system-level cybersecurity-related documentation.

d. Ensure that ISSOs are appointed in writing and provide oversight to ensure that they are following established cybersecurity policies and procedures.

e. Monitor compliance with cybersecurity policy, as appropriate, and review the results of such monitoring.

f. Ensure that cybersecurity inspections, tests, and reviews are synchronized and coordinated with affected parties and organizations.

g. Ensure implementation of IS security measures and procedures, including reporting incidents to the AO and appropriate reporting chains and coordinating system-level responses to unauthorized disclosures in accordance with Reference (bo) for classified information or Reference (bp) for CUI, respectively.

h. Ensure that the handling of possible or actual data spills of classified information resident in ISs, are conducted in accordance with Reference (bo).

i. Act as the primary cybersecurity technical advisor to the AO for DoD IS and PIT systems under their purview.

j. Ensure that cybersecurity-related events or configuration changes that may impact DoD IS and PIT systems authorization or security posture are formally reported to the AO and other affected parties, such as IOs and stewards and AOs of interconnected DoD ISs.

k. Ensure the secure configuration and approval of IT below the system level (i.e., products and IT services) in accordance with applicable guidance prior to acceptance into or connection to a DoD IS or PIT system.

19. INFORMATION SYSTEM SECURITY OFFICER (ISSO) (formerly known as IA Officers). When circumstances warrant, a single individual may fulfill both the ISSM and the ISSO roles. ISSOs:

a. Assist the ISSMs in meeting their duties and responsibilities.

b. Implement and enforce all DoD IS and PIT system cybersecurity policies and procedures, as defined by cybersecurity-related documentation.

c. Ensure that all users have the requisite security clearances and access authorization, and are aware of their cybersecurity responsibilities for DoD IS and PIT systems under their purview before being granted access to those systems.

d. In coordination with the ISSM, initiate protective or corrective measures when a cybersecurity incident or vulnerability is discovered and ensure that a process is in place for authorized users to report all cybersecurity-related events and potential threats and vulnerabilities to the ISSO.

e. Ensure that all DoD IS cybersecurity-related documentation is current and accessible to properly authorized individuals.

20. <u>PRIVILEGED USERS</u>. Privileged users (e.g., system administrators) must:

a. Configure and operate IT within the authorities vested in them according to DoD cybersecurity policies and procedures.

b. Notify the responsible ISSO or, in the absence of an ISSO, the responsible ISSM, of any changes that might affect security posture.

21. <u>AUTHORIZED USERS</u>. Authorized users must:

a. Immediately report all cybersecurity-related events (e.g., data spill) and potential threats and vulnerabilities (e.g., insider threat) to the appropriate ISSO or, in the absence of an ISSO, the ISSM.

b. Protect authenticators commensurate with the classification or sensitivity of the information accessed and report any compromise or suspected compromise of an authenticator to the appropriate ISSO.

c. Protect terminals, workstations, other input or output devices and resident data from unauthorized access.

d. Inform the responsible ISSO when access to a particular DoD IS or PIT system is no longer required (e.g., completion of project, transfer, retirement, resignation).

e. Observe policies and procedures governing the secure operation and authorized use of DoD IT, including operations security in accordance with Reference (dg) and DoDD 5205.02E (Reference (dy)).

f. Use DoD IT only for official or authorized purposes.

g. Not unilaterally bypass, strain, or test cybersecurity mechanisms. If cybersecurity mechanisms must be bypassed, users will coordinate the procedure with the ISSO and receive written approval from the ISSM.

h. Not introduce or use software, firmware, or hardware that has not been approved by the AO or a designated representative on DoD IT.

i. Not relocate or change DoD IT equipment or the network connectivity of equipment without proper authorization.

j. Meet minimum cybersecurity awareness requirements in accordance with Reference (ba).

GLOSSARY

PART I. ABBREVIATIONS AND ACRONYMS

AO	authorizing official
ASD(NII)	Assistant Secretary of Defense for Networks and Information Integration
ATO	authorization to operate
BIOS	basic input and output system
BMA	Business Mission Area
CCI	control correlation identifier
CD	cross-domain
CDS	cross-domain solution
CI	counterintelligence
CIO	Chief Information Officer
CJCS	Chairman of the Joint Chiefs of Staff
CJCSI	Chairman of the Joint Chiefs of Staff Instruction
CNSS	Committee on National Security Systems
CNSSI	Committee on National Security Systems Instruction
CNSSP	Committee on National Security Systems Policy
COMSEC	communications security
CSS	Central Security Service
CUI	controlled unclassified information
DASD(DT&E)	Deputy Assistant Secretary of Defense for Developmental Test and Evaluation
DCMO	Deputy Chief Management Office
DCPDS	Defense Civilian Personnel Data System
DIA	Defense Intelligence Agency
DIB	Defense Industrial Base
DIMA	DoD portion of the intelligence mission area
DIRNSA/CHCSS	Director, National Security Agency/Chief, Central Security Service
DISA	Defense Information Systems Agency
DISN	Defense Information Systems Network

DITPR	DoD Information Technology Portfolio Repository
DNI	Director of National Intelligence
DoD CIO	DoD Chief Information Officer
DoD ISRMC	DoD Information Security Risk Management Committee
DoDD	DoD directive
DoDI	DoD instruction
DoDIIS	DoD Intelligence Information System
DoDM	DoD manual
DOT&E	Director, Operational Test and Evaluation
DSAWG	Defense Information Assurance Security Accreditation Working Group
DSS	Defense Security Service
DT&E	Developmental Test and Evaluation
DTM	directive-type memorandum
EIEMA	enterprise information environment mission area
ESSG	Enterprise-wide Information Assurance and Computer Network Defense Solutions Steering Group
FN	foreign national
GIG	Global Information Grid
IA	information assurance
IASE	information assurance support environment
IC	Intelligence Community
IO	information owner
IS	information system
ISO	information system owner
ISSM	Information System Security Manager
ISSO	Information System Security Officer
IT	information technology
JWICS	Joint Worldwide Intelligence Communications System
KS	Knowledge Service

GLOSSARY

LE	law enforcement
LE/CI	law enforcement and counterintelligence
MA	mission area
NIPRNet	Non-Classified Internet Protocol Router Network
NIST	National Institute of Standards and Technology
NSA	National Security Agency
NSS	National Security System
OT&E	operational test and evaluation
PAO	principal authorizing official
PIA	privacy impact assessment
PII	personally identifiable information
PIT	platform information technology
PKI	public key infrastructure
PM	program manager
PPP	program protection plan
RMF	risk management framework
SAP	special access program
SAPCO	SAP Central Office
SCAP	security content automation protocol
SCI	sensitive compartmented information
SIPRNet	Secret Internet Protocol Router Network
SISO	Senior Information Security Officer
SITR	Secret Internet Protocol Router Network Information Technology Registry
SLA	Service-level agreement
SM	system manager
SP	Special Publication
SRG	security requirements guide
SSE	system security engineering
STIG	security technical implementation guide

GLOSSARY

T&E	test and evaluation
TPM	trusted platform module
TRANSEC	transmission security
TRMC	Test Resource Management Center
TSN	trusted systems and networks
UCDMO	Unified Cross Domain Management Office
U.S.C.	United States Code
USD(AT&L)	Under Secretary of Defense for Acquisition, Technology, and Logistics
USD(I)	Under Secretary of Defense for Intelligence
USD(P)	Under Secretary of Defense for Policy
USD(P&R)	Under Secretary of Defense for Personnel and Readiness
USSTRATCOM	United States Strategic Command

PART II. DEFINITIONS

Unless otherwise noted, these terms and their definitions are for the purposes of this instruction.

application. Defined in Reference (dz).

authenticator. Defined in Reference (dz).

authorized user. Defined in Reference (w).

availability. Defined in Reference (dz).

Blue Team. Defined in Reference (dz).

CCI. Decomposition of an NIST control into single, actionable, measurable statement.

confidentiality. Defined in Reference (dz).

continuous monitoring. Defined in Reference (cs).

cybersecurity. Prevention of damage to, protection of, and restoration of computers, electronic communications systems, electronic communications services, wire communication, and electronic communication, including information contained therein, to ensure its availability, integrity, authentication, confidentiality, and nonrepudiation. (Reference (m))

cybersecurity architect. See "Information Security Architect" definition in Reference (ch).

cyberspace. Defined in Reference (dz).

cyberspace defense. Actions normally created within DoD cyberspace for securing, operating, and defending the DoD information networks. Specific actions include protect, detect, characterize, counter, and mitigate.

DoD-controlled. Used only for DoD purposes, dedicated to DoD processing, and effectively under DoD configuration control.

DoD information. Any information that has not been cleared for public release in accordance with Reference (dc) and that has been collected, developed, received, transmitted, used, or stored by DoD, or by a non-DoD entity in support of an official DoD activity.

DoD Information Enterprise. Defined in Reference (r).

DoD IS. DoD-owned IS and DoD-controlled IS. A type of DoD IT.

DoD IT. DoD-owned IT and DoD-controlled IT. DoD IT includes IS, PIT, IT services, and IT products.

DoD-partnered systems. ISs or PIT systems that are developed jointly by DoD and non-DoD mission partners, comprise DoD and non-DoD ISs, or contain a mix of DoD and non-DoD information consumers and producers (e.g., jointly developed systems, multi-national or coalition environments, or first responder environments).

FN. Defined in Joint Publication 1-02 (Reference (ea)).

enclave. Defined in Reference (dz).

GIG. Defined in Reference (r).

identity assurance. See "assurance" definition in NIST SP 800-63 (Reference (eb)).

IA. Defined in Reference (dz).

IA and IA-enabled product. Defined in Reference (bg).

IO. Defined in Reference (dz).

information resource. Defined in Reference (dz).

information steward. Defined in Reference (dz).

insider threat. Defined in Reference (cv).

<u>integrity</u>. Defined in Reference (dz) as NIST SP 800-53 definition.

<u>IS</u>. Defined in Reference (dz).

<u>ISO</u>. Defined in Reference (ch), but for the purposes of this instruction is not synonymous with "PM" as indicated in Reference (ch).

<u>IS security engineer</u>. Defined in Reference (dz).

<u>ISSM</u>. Defined in Reference (dz).

<u>ISSO</u>. Defined in Reference (dz).

<u>IT</u>. Defined in Reference (dz).

<u>IT product</u>. Individual IT hardware or software items. Products can be commercial or government provided and include, but are not limited to, operating systems, office productivity software, firewalls, and routers.

<u>IT Service</u>. A capability provided to one or more DoD entities by an internal or external provider based on the use of information technology and that supports a DoD mission or business process. An IT Service consists of a combination of people, processes, and technology.

<u>key management infrastructure</u>. Defined in Reference (dz).

<u>major application</u>. An application that requires special attention to security due to the risk and magnitude of the harm resulting from the loss, misuse, or unauthorized access to or modification of the information in the application. All federal applications require some level of protection. Certain applications, because of the information in them, however, require special management oversight and should be treated as major. Adequate security for other applications should be provided by security of the systems in which they operate. (Reference (al))

<u>MA</u>. Defined in Reference (ac).

<u>mission partners</u>. Defined in Reference (r).

<u>mobile code</u>. Defined in Reference (dz).

<u>mobile code risk categories</u>. Categories of risk associated with mobile code technology based on functionality, level of access to workstation, server, and remote system services and resources, and the resulting threat to information systems.

<u>NSS</u>. Defined in Reference (dz).

<u>network</u>. Defined in Reference (dz).

operational resilience. The ability of systems to resist, absorb, and recover from or adapt to an adverse occurrence during operation that may cause harm, destruction, or loss of ability to perform mission-related functions.

overlay. Defined in Reference (ci).

PIA. Defined in Reference (de).

PIT. IT, both hardware and software, that is physically part of, dedicated to, or essential in real time to the mission performance of special purpose systems.

PIT system. A collection of PIT within an identified boundary under the control of a single authority and security policy. The systems may be structured by physical proximity or by function, independent of location.

policy interoperability. Common business processes related to the transmission, receipt, and acceptance of data among participants.

privileged user. Defined in Reference (dz).

private DoD internet service. Defined in Reference (dh).

PM or SM. The individual with responsibility for and authority to accomplish program or system objectives for development, production, and sustainment to meet the user's operational needs.

PPP. Defined in Reference (ay).

public key enabling. Defined in Reference (dz).

reciprocity. Defined in Reference (dz).

Red Team. Defined in Reference (dz).

risk executive function. Defined in Reference (dz).

security category. Defined in Reference (dz).

security control assessor. Defined in Reference (ch).

security controls. Defined in Reference (dz).

security posture. Defined in Reference (dz).

semantic interoperability. The ability of each sending party to communicate data and have receiving parties understand the message in the sense intended by the sending party.

SISO. See "Senior (Agency) Information Security Officer" definition in Reference (ch). The SISO role, as described in law (Reference (aa)) and by NIST, should not be confused with information security roles and responsibilities within References (bo), (bp), (bs), (by), and (cz).

SRG. Compilation of CCIs grouped in more applicable, specific technology areas at various levels of technology and product specificity. Contain all requirements that have been flagged as applicable from the parent level regardless if they are selected on a DoD baseline or not.

SSE. See "IS security engineering" definition in Reference (dz).

stand-alone system. System that is not connected to any other network and does not transmit, receive, route, or exchange information outside of the system's authorization boundary.

STIG. Based on DoD policy and security controls. Implementation guide geared to a specific product and version. Contains all requirements that have been flagged as applicable for the product which have been selected on a DoD baseline.

supply chain risk. Defined in Reference (bm).

system development life cycle. Defined in Reference (dz).

technical interoperability. The ability for different technologies to communicate and exchange data based on well-defined and widely adopted interface standards.

TEMPEST. Defined in Reference (dz).

TRANSEC. Defined in Reference (dz).

TPM. The TPM is a microcontroller that stores keys, passwords, and digital certificates. It typically is affixed to the motherboard of computers. It potentially can be used in any computing device that requires these functions. The nature of this hardware chip ensures that the information stored there is made more secure from external software attack and physical theft. The TPM standard is a product of the Trusted Computing Group consortium. For more information on the TPM specification and architecture, refer to www.trustedcomputinggroup.org/groups/tpm.

UCDMO CDS Baseline List. A list managed by the UCDMO that identifies CDSs that are available for deployment within the DoD and IC.

UCDMO CDS Sunset List. A list managed by the UCDMO that identifies CDSs that are or have been in operation but are no longer available for additional deployment and need to be replaced within a specified period of time.

CyberSecurity Standards Library™

NIST SP 500-288	Specification for WS-Biometric Devices (WS-BD)
NIST SP 500-291 V2	NIST Cloud Computing Standards Roadmap
NIST SP 500-292	NIST Cloud Computing Reference Architecture
NIST SP 500-293 V1 & V2	US Government Cloud Computing Technology Roadmap
NIST SP 500-293 V3	US Government Cloud Computing Technology Roadmap
NIST SP 500-299	NIST Cloud Computing Security Reference Architecture
NIST SP 500-304	Data Format for the Interchange of Fingerprint, Facial & Other Biometric Information
NIST SP 800-1	Bibliography of Selected Computer Security Publications January 1980-October 1989
NIST SP 800-12 R1	An Introduction to Information Security
NIST SP 800-13	Telecommunications Security Guidelines for Telecommunications Management Network
NIST SP 800-14	Generally Accepted Principles and Practices for Securing Information Technology Systems
NIST SP 800-15 V1	Minimum Interoperability Specification for PKI Components (MISPC)
NIST SP 800-16 R1	A Role-Based Model for Federal Information Technology/Cybersecurity Training
NIST SP 800-17	Modes of Operation Validation System (MOVS): Requirements and Procedures
NIST SP 800-18 R1	Developing Security Plans for Federal Information Systems
NIST SP 800-19	Mobile Agent Security
NIST SP 800-20	Modes of Operation Validation System for the Triple Data Encryption Algorithm
NIST SP 800-22 R1a	A Statistical Test Suite for Random and Pseudorandom Number Generators for Cryptographic Applications
NIST SP 800-23	Guidelines to Federal Organizations on Security Assurance and Acquisition/Use of Tested/Evaluated Products
NIST SP 800-24	PBX Vulnerability Analysis - Finding Holes in Your PBX Before Someone Else Does
NIST SP 800-25	Federal Agency Use of Public Key Technology for Digital Signatures and Authentication
NIST SP 800-27 Rev A	Engineering Principles for Information Technology Security (A Baseline for Achieving Security)
NIST SP 800-28	Guidelines on Active Content and Mobile Code
NIST SP 800-29	A Comparison of the Security Requirements for Cryptographic Modules in FIPS 140-1 and FIPS 140-2
NIST SP 800-30	Guide for Conducting Risk Assessments
NIST SP 800-31	Intrusion Detection Systems
NIST SP 800-32	Public Key Technology and the Federal PKI Infrastructure
NIST SP 800-33	Underlying Technical Models for Information Technology Security
NIST SP 800-34 R1	Contingency Planning Guide for Federal Information Systems
NIST SP 800-35	Guide to Information Technology Security Services
NIST SP 800-36	Guide to Selecting Information Technology Security Products
NIST SP 800-37 R2	Applying Risk Management Framework to Federal Information
NIST SP 800-38	Recommendation for Block Cipher Modes of Operation
NIST SP 800-38A Addendum	Block Cipher Modes of Operation: Three Variants of Ciphertext Stealing for CBC Mode
NIST SP 800-38B	Block Cipher Modes of Operation: The CMAC Mode for Authentication
NIST SP 800-38C	Block Cipher Modes of Operation: The CCM Mode for Authentication and Confidentiality
NIST SP 800-38D	Block Cipher Modes of Operation: Galois/Counter Mode (GCM) and GMAC
NIST SP 800-38E	Block Cipher Modes of Operation: The XTS-AES Mode for Confidentiality on Storage Devices
NIST SP 800-38F	Block Cipher Modes of Operation: Methods for Key Wrapping
NIST SP 800-38G	Block Cipher Modes of Operation: Methods for Format-Preserving Encryption
NIST SP 800-39	Managing Information Security Risk
NIST SP 800-40 R3	Guide to Enterprise Patch Management Technologies
NIST SP 800-41	Guidelines on Firewalls and Firewall Policy
NIST SP 800-43	Systems Administration Guidance for Securing Microsoft Windows 2000 Professional System
NIST SP 800-44 V2	Guidelines on Securing Public Web Servers
NIST SP 800-45 V2	Guidelines on Electronic Mail Security
NIST SP 800-46 R2	Guide to Enterprise Telework, Remote Access, and Bring Your Own Device (BYOD) Security
NIST SP 800-47	Security Guide for Interconnecting Information Technology Systems
NIST SP 800-48	Guide to Securing Legacy IEEE 802.11 Wireless Networks
NIST SP 800-49	Federal S/MIME V3 Client Profile
NIST SP 800-50	Building an Information Technology Security Awareness and Training Program
NIST SP 800-51 R1	Guide to Using Vulnerability Naming Schemes
NIST SP 800-52 R1	Guidelines for the Selection, Configuration, and Use of Transport Layer Security (TLS) Implementations
NIST SP 800-53 R5	Security and Privacy Controls for Information Systems and Organizations
NIST SP 800-53A R4	Assessing Security and Privacy Controls
NIST SP 800-54	Border Gateway Protocol Security
NIST SP 800-55 R1	Performance Measurement Guide for Information Security
NIST SP 800-56A R3	Pair-Wise Key-Establishment Schemes Using Discrete Logarithm Cryptography
NIST SP 56B R 1	Recommendation for Pair-Wise Key-Establishment Schemes Using Integer Factorization Cryptography
NIST SP 800-56C R1	Recommendation for Key-Derivation Methods in Key-Establishment Schemes - Draft
NIST SP 800-57 R4	Recommendation for Key Management
NIST SP 800-58	Security Considerations for Voice Over IP Systems
NIST SP 800-59	Guideline for Identifying an Information System as a National Security System
NIST SP 800-60	Guide for Mapping Types of Information and Information Systems to Security Categories
NIST SP 800-61 R2	Computer Security Incident Handling Guide
NIST SP 800-63-3	Digital Identity Guidelines
NIST SP 800-63a	Digital Identity Guidelines - Enrollment and Identity Proofing
NIST SP 800-63b	Digital Identity Guidelines - Authentication and Lifecycle Management
NIST SP 800-63c	Digital Identity Guidelines- Federation and Assertions
NIST SP 800-64 R2	Security Considerations in the System Development Life Cycle

Click on a title to obtain a printed copy of these standards at Amazon.com

CyberSecurity Standards Library™

NIST SP 800-65	Integrating IT Security into the Capital Planning and Investment Control Process
NIST SP 800-66	Implementing the Health Insurance Portability and Accountability Act (HIPAA) Security Rule
NIST SP 800-67 R2	Recommendation for Triple Data Encryption Algorithm (TDEA) Block Cipher - Draft
NIST SP 800-68 R1	Guide to Securing Microsoft Windows XP Systems for IT Professionals: A NIST Security Configuration Checklist
NIST SP 800-69	Guidance for Securing Microsoft Windows XP Home Edition: A NIST Security Configuration Checklist
NIST SP 800-70 R4	National Checklist Program for IT Products
NIST SP 800-72	Guidelines on PDA Forensics
NIST SP 800-73-4	Interfaces for Personal Identity Verification
NIST SP 800-76-2	Biometric Specifications for Personal Identity Verification
NIST SP 800-77	Guide to IPsec VPNs
NIST SP 800-78-4	Cryptographic Algorithms and Key Sizes for Personal Identity Verification
NIST SP 800-79-2	Authorization of Personal Identity Verification Card Issuers (PCI) and Derived PIV Credential Issuers (DPCI)
NIST SP 800-81-2	Secure Domain Name System (DNS) Deployment Guide
NIST SP 800-82 R2	Guide to Industrial Control Systems (ICS) Security
NIST SP 800-83	Guide to Malware Incident Prevention and Handling for Desktops and Laptops
NIST SP 800-84	Guide to Test, Training, and Exercise Programs for IT Plans and Capabilities
NIST SP 800-85A-4 PIV	Card Application and Middleware Interface Test Guidelines
NIST SP 800-85B-4 PIV	Data Model Test Guidelines - Draft
NIST SP 800-86	Guide to Integrating Forensic Techniques into Incident Response
NIST SP 800-87 R1	Codes for Identification of Federal and Federally-Assisted Organizations
NIST SP 800-88 R1	Guidelines for Media Sanitization
NIST SP 800-89	Recommendation for Obtaining Assurances for Digital Signature Applications
NIST SP 800-90A R1	Random Number Generation Using Deterministic Random Bit Generators
NIST SP 800-90B	Recommendation for the Entropy Sources Used for Random Bit Generation
NIST SP 800-90C	Recommendation for Random Bit Generator (RBG) Constructions - 2nd Draft
NIST SP 800-92	Guide to Computer Security Log Management
NIST SP 800-94	Guide to Intrusion Detection and Prevention Systems (IDPS)
NIST SP 800-95	Guide to Secure Web Services
NIST SP 800-97	Establishing Wireless Robust Security Networks: A Guide to IEEE 802.11i
NIST SP 800-98	Guidelines for Securing Radio Frequency Identification (RFID) Systems
NIST SP 800-100	Information Security Handbook: A Guide for Managers
NIST SP 800-101 R1	Guidelines on Mobile Device Forensics
NIST SP 800-102	Recommendation for Digital Signature Timeliness
NIST SP 800-106	Randomized Hashing for Digital Signatures
NIST SP 800-107 R1	Recommendation for Applications Using Approved Hash Algorithms
NIST SP 800-108	Recommendation for Key Derivation Using Pseudorandom Functions
NIST SP 800-111	Guide to Storage Encryption Technologies for End User Devices
NIST SP 800-113	Guide to SSL VPNs
NIST SP 800-114 R1	User's Guide to Telework and Bring Your Own Device (BYOD) Security
NIST SP 800-115	Technical Guide to Information Security Testing and Assessment
NIST SP 800-116	A Recommendation for the Use of PIV Credentials in PACS - Draft
NIST SP 800-117 V1.2	Guide to Adopting and Using the Security Content Automation Protocol (SCAP) - Draft
NIST SP 800-119	Guidelines for the Secure Deployment of IPv6
NIST SP 800-120	Recommendation for EAP Methods Used in Wireless Network Access Authentication
NIST SP 800-121 R2	Guide to Bluetooth Security
NIST SP 800-122	Guide to Protecting the Confidentiality of Personally Identifiable Information
NIST SP 800-123	Guide to General Server Security
NIST SP 800-124 R1	Managing the Security of Mobile Devices in the Enterprise
NIST SP 800-125 (A & B)	Secure Virtual Network Configuration for Virtual Machine (VM) Protection
NIST SP 800-126 R3	Technical Specification for the Security Content Automation Protocol (SCAP)
NIST SP 800-126A	SCAP 1.3 Component Specification 3 Version Updates
NIST SP 800-127	Guide to Securing WiMAX Wireless Communications
NIST SP 800-128	Guide for Security-Focused Configuration Management of Information Systems
NIST SP 800-130	A Framework for Designing Cryptographic Key Management Systems
NIST SP 800-131A R1	Transitions: Recommendation for Transitioning the Use of Cryptographic Algorithms and Key Lengths
NIST SP 800-132	Recommendation for Password-Based Key Derivation - Part 1: Storage Applications
NIST SP 800-133	Recommendation for Cryptographic Key Generation
NIST SP 800-135 R1	Recommendation for Existing Application-Specific Key Derivation Functions
NIST SP 800-137	Information Security Continuous Monitoring (ISCM)
NIST SP 800-142	Practical Combinatorial Testing
NIST SP 800-144	Guidelines on Security and Privacy in Public Cloud Computing
NIST SP 800-145	The NIST Definition of Cloud Computing
NIST SP 800-146	Cloud Computing Synopsis and Recommendations
NIST SP 800-147	BIOS Protection Guidelines & BIOS Integrity Measurement Guidelines
NIST SP 800-147B	BIOS Protection Guidelines for Servers
NIST SP 800-150	Guide to Cyber Threat Information Sharing
NIST SP 800-152	A Profile for U.S. Federal Cryptographic Key Management Systems
NIST SP 800-153	Guidelines for Securing Wireless Local Area Networks (WLANs)
NIST SP 800-154	Guide to Data-Centric System Threat Modeling

Click on a title to obtain a printed copy of these standards at Amazon.com

CyberSecurity Standards Library™

NIST SP 800-155	BIOS Integrity Measurement Guidelines
NIST SP 800-156	Representation of PIV Chain-of-Trust for Import and Export
NIST SP 800-157	Guidelines for Derived Personal Identity Verification (PIV) Credentials
NIST SP 800-160	Systems Security Engineering
NIST SP 800-161	Supply Chain Risk Management Practices for Federal Information Systems and Organizations
NIST SP 800-162	Guide to Attribute Based Access Control (ABAC) Definition and Considerations
NIST SP 800-163	Vetting the Security of Mobile Applications
NIST SP 800-164	Guidelines on Hardware- Rooted Security in Mobile Devices Draft
NIST SP 800-166	Derived PIV Application and Data Model Test Guidelines
NIST SP 800-167	Guide to Application Whitelisting
NIST SP 800-168	Approximate Matching: Definition and Terminology
NIST SP 800-171 R1	Protecting Controlled Unclassified Information in Nonfederal Systems
NIST SP 800-175 (A & B)	Guideline for Using Cryptographic Standards in the Federal Government
NIST SP 800-177 R1	Trustworthy Email
NIST SP 800-178	Comparison of Attribute Based Access Control (ABAC) Standards for Data Service Applications
NIST SP 800-179	Guide to Securing Apple OS X 10.10 Systems for IT Professional
NIST SP 800-180	NIST Definition of Microservices, Application Containers and System Virtual Machines
NIST SP 800-181	National Initiative for Cybersecurity Education (NICE) Cybersecurity Workforce Framework
NIST SP 800-183	Networks of 'Things'
NIST SP 800-184	Guide for Cybersecurity Event Recovery
NIST SP 800-185	SHA-3 Derived Functions: cSHAKE, KMAC, TupleHash and ParallelHash
NIST SP 800-187	Guide to LTE Security - Draft
NIST SP 800-188	De-Identifying Government Datasets - (2nd Draft)
NIST SP 800-190	Application Container Security Guide
NIST SP 800-191	The NIST Definition of Fog Computing
NIST SP 800-192	Verification and Test Methods for Access Control Policies/Models
NIST SP 800-193	Platform Firmware Resiliency Guidelines
NIST SP 1800-1	Securing Electronic Health Records on Mobile Devices
NIST SP 1800-2	Identity and Access Management for Electric Utilities 1800-2a & 1800-2b
NIST SP 1800-2	Identity and Access Management for Electric Utilities 1800-2c
NIST SP 1800-3	Attribute Based Access Control NIST 1800-3a & 3b
NIST SP 1800-3	Attribute Based Access Control NIST 1800-3c Chapters 1 - 6
NIST SP 1800-3	Attribute Based Access Control NIST1800-3c Chapters 7 - 10
NIST SP 1800-4a & 4b	Mobile Device Security: Cloud and Hybrid Builds
NIST SP 1800-4c	Mobile Device Security: Cloud and Hybrid Builds
NIST SP 1800-5	IT Asset Management: Financial Services
NIST SP 1800-6	Domain Name Systems-Based Electronic Mail Security
NIST SP 1800-7	Situational Awareness for Electric Utilities
NIST SP 1800-8	Securing Wireless Infusion Pumps
NIST SP 1800-9a & 9b	Access Rights Management for the Financial Services Sector
NIST SP 1800-9c	Access Rights Management for the Financial Services Sector - How To Guide
NIST SP 1800-11a & 11b	Data Integrity Recovering from Ransomware and Other Destructive Events
NIST SP 1800-11c	Data Integrity Recovering from Ransomware and Other Destructive Events - How To Guide
NIST SP 1800-12	Derived Personal Identity Verification (PIV) Credentials
NISTIR 7100	PDA Forensic Tools: An Overview and Analysis
NISTIR 7188	Specification for the Extensible Configuration Checklist Description Format (XCCDF)
NISTIR 7200	Proximity Beacons and Mobile Device Authentication: An Overview and Implementation
NISTIR 7206	Smart Cards and Mobile Device Authentication: An Overview and Implementation
NISTIR 7250	Cell Phone Forensic Tools: An Overview and Analysis
NISTIR 7275 V1.1	Specification for the Extensible Configuration Checklist Description Format (XCCDF)
NISTIR 7275 R4 V1.2	Specification for the Extensible Configuration Checklist Description Format (XCCDF)
NISTIR 7284	Personal Identity Verification Card Management Report
NISTIR 7290	Fingerprint Identification and Mobile Handheld Devices: An Overview and Implementation
NISTIR 7298 R2	Glossary of Key Information Security Terms
NISTIR 7316	Assessment of Access Control Systems
NISTIR 7337	Personal Identity Verification Demonstration Summary
NISTIR 7358	Program Review for Information Security Management Assistance (PRISMA)
NISTIR 7359	Information Security Guide for Government Executives
NISTIR 7387	Cell Phone Forensic Tools: An Overview and Analysis Update
NISTIR 7435	The Common Vulnerability Scoring System (CVSS) and Its Applicability to Federal Agency Systems
NISTIR 7452	Secure Biometric Match-on-Card Feasibility Report
NISTIR 7497	Security Architecture Design Process for Health Information Exchanges (HIEs)
NISTIR 7502	The Common Configuration Scoring System (CCSS): Metrics for Software Security Configuration Vulnerabilities
NISTIR 7511 R4 V1.2	Security Content Automation Protocol (SCAP) Version 1.2 Validation Program Test Requirements
NISTIR 7516	Forensic Filtering of Cell Phone Protocols
NISTIR 7539	Symmetric Key Injection onto Smart Cards
NISTIR 7551	A Threat Analysis on UOCAVA Voting Systems
NISTIR 7559	Forensics Web Services (FWS)
NISTIR 7564	Directions in Security Metrics Research
NISTIR 7581	System and Network Security Acronyms and Abbreviations

Click on a title to obtain a printed copy of these standards at Amazon.com

CyberSecurity Standards Library™

NISTIR 7601	Framework for Emergency Response Officials (ERO)
NISTIR 7611	Use of ISO/IEC 24727
NISTIR 7617	Mobile Forensic Reference Materials: A Methodology and Reification
NISTIR 7621 R1	Small Business Information Security: The Fundamentals
NISTIR 7622	Notional Supply Chain Risk Management Practices for Federal Information Systems
NISTIR 7628 R1 Vol 1	Guidelines for Smart Grid Cybersecurity - Architecture, and High-Level Requirements
NISTIR 7628 R1 Vol 2	Guidelines for Smart Grid Cybersecurity - Privacy and the Smart Grid
NISTIR 7628 R1 Vol 3	Guidelines for Smart Grid Cybersecurity - Supportive Analyses and References
NISTIR 7658	Guide to SIMfill Use and Development
NISTIR 7676	Maintaining and Using Key History on Personal Identity Verification (PIV) Cards
NISTIR 7682	Information System Security Best Practices for UOCAVA-Supporting Systems
NISTIR 7692 V2	Specification for the Open Checklist Interactive Language (OCIL)
NISTIR 7693	Specification for Asset Identification 1.1
NISTIR 7694	Specification for the Asset Reporting Format 1.1
NISTIR 7696 V2.3	Common Platform Enumeration: Name Matching Specification
NISTIR 7697 V2.3	Common Platform Enumeration: Dictionary Specification
NISTIR 7698 V2.3	Common Platform Enumeration: Applicability Language Specification
NISTIR 7711	Security Best Practices for the Electronic Transmission of Election Materials for UOCAVA Voters
NISTIR 7756	CAESARS Framework Extension: An Enterprise Continuous Monitoring Technical Refer
NISTIR 7764	Status Report on the Second Round of the SHA-3 Cryptographic Hash Algorithm Competition
NISTIR 7770	Security Considerations for Remote Electronic UOCAVA Voting
NISTIR 7771 V2	Conformance Test Architecture for Biometric Data Interchange Formats - Beta
NISTIR 7773	An Application of Combinatorial Methods to Conformance Testing for Document Object Model Events
NISTIR 7788	Security Risk Analysis of Enterprise Networks Using Probabilistic Attack Graphs
NISTIR 7791	Conformance Test Architecture and Test Suite for ANSI/NIST-ITL 1-2007
NISTIR 7799	Continuous Monitoring Reference Model, Workflow, and Specifications - Draft
NISTIR 7800	Applying the Continuous Monitoring Technical Reference Model to the Asset, Configuration, and Vulnerability Management Domains - Draft
NISTIR 7823	Advanced Metering Infrastructure Smart Meter Upgradeability Test Framework
NISTIR 7874	Guidelines for Access Control System Evaluation Metrics
NISTIR 7904	Trusted Geolocation in the Cloud: Proof of Concept Implementation
NISTIR 7924	Reference Certificate Policy
NISTIR 7987	Policy Machine: Features, Architecture, and Specification
NISTIR 8006	NIST Cloud Computing Forensic Science Challenges
NISTIR 8011 Vol 1	Automation Support for Security Control Assessments
NISTIR 8011 Vol 2	Automation Support for Security Control Assessments
NISTIR 8040	Measuring the Usability and Security of Permuted Passwords on Mobile Platforms
NISTIR 8053	De-Identification of Personal Information
NISTIR 8054	NSTIC Pilots: Catalyzing the Identity Ecosystem
NISTIR 8055	Derived Personal Identity Verification (PIV) Credentials (DPC) Proof of Concept Research
NISTIR 8060	Guidelines for the Creation of Interoperable Software Identification (SWID) Tags
NISTIR 8062	Introduction to Privacy Engineering and Risk Management in Federal Systems
NISTIR 8074 Vol 1 & Vol 2	Strategic U.S. Government Engagement in International Standardization to Achieve U.S. Objectives for Cybersecurity
NISTIR 8080	Usability and Security Considerations for Public Safety Mobile Authentication
NISTIR 8089	An Industrial Control System Cybersecurity Performance Testbed
NISTIR 8112	Attribute Metadata - Draft
NISTIR 8135	Identifying and Categorizing Data Types for Public Safety Mobile Applications
NISTIR 8138	Vulnerability Description Ontology (VDO)
NISTIR 8144	Assessing Threats to Mobile Devices & Infrastructure
NISTIR 8151	Dramatically Reducing Software Vulnerabilities
NISTIR 8170	The Cybersecurity Framework
NISTIR 8176	Security Assurance Requirements for Linux Application Container Deployments
NISTIR 8179	Criticality Analysis Process Model
NISTIR 8183	Cybersecurity Framework Manufacturing Profile
NISTIR 8192	Enhancing Resilience of the Internet and Communications Ecosystem
Whitepaper	Cybersecurity Framework Manufacturing Profile
Whitepaper	NIST Framework for Improving Critical Infrastructure Cybersecurity
Whitepaper	Challenging Security Requirements for US Government Cloud Computing Adoption
FIPS PUBS 140-2	Security Requirements for Cryptographic Modules
FIPS PUBS 140-2 Annex A	Approved Security Functions
FIPS PUBS 140-2 Annex B	Approved Protection Profiles
FIPS PUBS 140-2 Annex C	Approved Random Number Generators
FIPS PUBS 140-2 Annex D	Approved Key Establishment Techniques
FIPS PUBS 180-4	Secure Hash Standard (SHS)
FIPS PUBS 186-4	Digital Signature Standard (DSS)
FIPS PUBS 197	Advanced Encryption Standard (AES)
FIPS PUBS 198-1	The Keyed-Hash Message Authentication Code (HMAC)
FIPS PUBS 199	Standards for Security Categorization of Federal Information and Information Systems
FIPS PUBS 200	Minimum Security Requirements for Federal Information and Information Systems

Click on a title to obtain a printed copy of these standards at Amazon.com

CyberSecurity Standards Library™

FIPS PUBS 201-2	Personal Identity Verification (PIV) of Federal Employees and Contractors
FIPS PUBS 202	SHA-3 Standard: Permutation-Based Hash and Extendable-Output Functions

DHS Study   DHS Study on Mobile Device Security

OMB A-130 / FISMA OMB A-130/Federal Information Security Modernization Act

DoD
UFC 3-430-11	Boiler Control Systems
UFC 4-010-06	Cybersecurity of Facility-Related Control Systems
FC 4-141-05N	Navy and Marine Corps Industrial Control Systems Monitoring Stations
MIL-HDBK-232A	RED/BLACK Engineering-Installation Guidelines
MIL-HDBK 1195	Radio Frequency Shielded Enclosures
TM 5-601	Supervisory Control and Data Acquisition (SCADA) Systems for C4ISR Facilities
ESTCP	Facility-Related Control Systems Cybersecurity Guideline
ESTCP	Facility-Related Control Systems Ver 4.0
DoD	Self-Assessing Security Vulnerabilities & Risks of Industrial Controls
DoD	Program Manager's Guidebook for Integrating the Cybersecurity Risk Management Framework (RMF) into the System Acquisition Lifecycle
DoD	Advanced Cyber Industrial Control System Tactics, Techniques, and Procedures (ACI TTP)

NERC
NERC CIP 002-5.1	Cyber Security — BES Cyber System Categorization
NERC CIP 003-6	Cyber Security — Security Management Controls
NERC CIP 003-7(i)	Cyber Security — Security Management Controls
NERC CIP 004-6	Cyber Security — Personnel & Training
NERC CIP 005-5	Cyber Security — Electronic Security Perimeter(s)
NERC CIP 006-6	Cyber Security — Physical Security of BES Cyber Systems
NERC CIP 007-6	Cyber Security — Systems Security Management
NERC CIP 008-5	Cyber Security — Incident Reporting and Response Planning
NERC CIP 009-6	Cyber Security — Recovery Plans for BES Cyber Systems
NERC CIP 010-2	Cyber Security — Configuration Change Management and Vulnerability
NERC CIP 011-2	Cyber Security — Information Protection
NERC CIP 014-2	Physical Security